Also by Frank Chodorov:
THE INCOME TAX: Root of All Evil
ONE IS A CROWD: Reflections of an Individualist

To Francine

When you are old enough to read this book there will be a Society and there will be a State, and both will take their character from the reigning ideas of the times. I suspect that these ideas, planted in the American mind before you were born, will be so different from those expressed in this book that you may have some difficulty in understanding how your grandfather "got that way." That could provide you with some good, clean fun—trying to reconstruct a long-lost pattern of thought.

Foreword

IT IS HARD to think of an age which, with less reason, has been more smugly self-satisfied than ours. The orthodoxies of the most solidly established high religious ages, founded as they were upon a belief in the transcendent sources of truth, have always been safeguarded by their very belief in the transcendent from the idolatry of man's worship of himself and his established habits. The power of kings and the pride of prelates remained intrinsically limited by the common acceptance of truths to which all men were subject. So when abuses proliferated and prophets arose to condemn the growth of power and the distortion of dogma, though their way was hard, they could appeal to fundamental beliefs to which everyone adhered.

But in our society, where relativism rules supreme, where truth is not merely distorted but its very existence denied, power grows to monstrous proportions without any inner check in the bosoms of those who hold it. In place of truth, the ideal is adjustment, that is, the acceptance of whatever happen to be the modes of thought and action established among us—not because it is purported that they are true, but just because they are. In this paradise for power unchecked by any criterion but its own, the way of the man who would bear witness to and fight for truth because it is truth is doubly hard. Not only, as in former ages, must he confront the established authorities of the day with the divergence of their acts from the demands of truth; he has to substantiate—explicitly or implicitly—the very title of truth as criterion.

This is the road Frank Chodorov has chosen. As essayist and as editor, on the lecture platform and in his personal influence upon those around him, he has devoted himself to a single end: to bear witness against that worship of the collective which is the omnipresent political error of the 20th century, and to vindicate the primary value of the individual person as the foundation from which all political thought and action derives its meaning.

His firm defense of the value of the individual person is in turn based upon his insistence on the validity of objective truth, of the Natural Law as source and criterion of right and wrong in the relations among men. This, in the atmosphere of the day, is adding insult to injury. Not content with attacking the dominant contemporary assumption that the collective "people," as represented by the state, is the moral center of human existence, infinitely superior to any mere individual person, he strikes at the same time at the positivism and the pragmatism that have made it possible for this assumption to take root and grow.

Frank Chodorov has devoted the whole of his mature life to a struggle against the twin perversions of concentrated power in the state and intellectual irresponsibility in the academy. As editor of *The Freeman, Analysis*, and *Human Events*, in his multifarious writings and speeches, in his books—*One Is a Crowd* and *The Income Tax: Root of All Evil*—he has never ceased to hammer away at his essential theme: the danger of concentrated power to the freedom of individual human beings. One does not have to agree with him on every aspect of his analysis, or with all his proposals, to recognize that his voice is one of the few clear voices of freedom speaking today. He has truly something of the prophet about him—not the hortatory prophet, but the quiet speaker of parables.

Now in his seventies, he gives us in this book a vigorous and compelling epitome of his beliefs. The sentence with which it ends, "The will for freedom comes before freedom," reflects his purpose and underlines his achievement. For to the re-awakening of the will to freedom and the understanding of freedom, Frank Chodorov has contributed mightily.

FRANK S. MEYER

Acknowledgment

THIS ESSAY is the result of conversations with Albert Jay Nock, author of *Our Enemy the State*, some fifteen years ago. His book was then out of print and the publishers were considering a reissue; for commercial reasons they held that it should be expanded. I had been suggesting to him the need of revision and expansion for quite another reason. The book was based on a series of lectures delivered to a graduate class in history, and on that account it dealt with the State historically; my argument was that it could be handled as an economic phenomenon and that the inclusion of this phase would broaden the scope of the book. Something of a joint venture along this line was under consideration at the time of Nock's death.

I mention this fact to ward off the charge of plagiarism. For, as any reader of *Our Enemy the State* will readily recognize, I have borrowed ideas from it quite liberally in the writing of this essay. I plead the circumstance related above as my justification. Knowing Nock, I am sure that he would be the last to take me to task for appropriating some of his argument, and would be quick to point out that originality is a fiction and a posture.

The fact is, I am under obligation to many writers of economics and political science; traces of a half century of reading have found their way into this book. Why, then, did I not acknowledge my debt to these writers in a formal way, with annotations and a bibliography? Partly because this would have entailed a lot of drudgery, with nothing more to show for it than a few extra pages of print, and partly because this method of drawing upon authorities for sup-port has always struck me as special pleading, spurious and slightly dishonest.

When an author refers the reader to a previous author, in an annotation, he is really saying: "This is not my idea, it is what an established authority has said on the subject and ought therefore to be accepted without question." But, as every exponent of a theory knows, one can draw upon authorities to support either side of a case, just as lawyers do with precedents, and it is natural for a protagonist to cite only those authorities who support his thesis; if he cites a contrary-minded authority, it is only to set him up for demolition. Only a gullible reader, or one who was convinced before he took up the book, will be impressed by this shoring up of argument.

This book lays no claim to being authoritative or original. Its ideas have been borrowed, mostly in an unconscious way, from the goodly number of writers whose thinking appealed to me. This is my blanket acknowledgment to all of them. The best that can be said of my effort is that it is an arrangement of their ideas in a way that will support the conviction I had before I started writing. If the reader finds the book interesting it is mainly because he was attuned to the line of thought to begin with; if the "furniture of his mind" is otherwise arranged, he will probably not finish reading it. The first, if stimulated, will be prompted to dig into a library to find out how I "got that way"; the other would hardly check up on any bibliography I might have added.

FRANK CHODOROV

Berkeley Heights, N. J.
January 1959

Contents

Foreword by Frank S. Meyer   5

Acknowledgment   7

Introduction   10

1.   Economics Versus Politics   15
2.   From God or the Sword?   20
3.   The Unit of Social Life   26
4.   Society Are People   32
5.   "Easy Come, Easy Go"   38
6.   The Humanity of Trade   45
7.   Plenty by Competition   51
8.   Government and Property   57
9.   A Case of Corruption   66
10.   A State is Born   72
11.   "Social Services"   79
12.   The Profit of Reform   87
13.   The Maker of Shortages   95
14.   A Matter of Degree   103
15.   One Can Always Hope   110

Introduction

WHAT HISTORY will think of our times is something that only history will tell. But it is a good guess that it will select collectivism as the identifying characteristic of the twentieth century. For, even a quick survey of the developing pattern of thought during the past fifty years shows up the dominance of one central idea: that Society is a transcendent entity, something apart from and greater than the sum of its parts, possessing a suprahuman character and endowed with like capacities. It operates in a field of its own, ethically and philosophically, and is guided by stars unknown to mortals. Hence, the individual, the unit of Society, cannot judge it by his own limitations nor apply to it standards by which he measures his own thinking and behavior. He is necessary to it, of course, but only as a replaceable part of a machine. It follows, therefore, that Society, which may concern itself paternalistically with individuals, is in no way dependent on them.

In one way or another, this idea has insinuated itself into almost every branch of thought and, as ideas have a way of doing, has become institutionalized. Perhaps the most glaring example is the modern orientation of the philosophy of education. Many of the professionals in this field frankly assert that the primary purpose of education is not to develop the individual's capacity for learning, as was held in the past, but to prepare him for a fruitful and "happy" place in Society; his inclinations must be turned away from himself, so that he can drop into the *mores* of his age group and beyond that into the social milieu in which he will live out his life. He is not an end in himself.

Jurisprudence has come around to the same idea, holding more and more that human behavior is not a matter of personal responsibility as much as it is a reflection of the social forces working on the individual; the tendency is to lay on Society the blame for crimes committed by its members. This, too, is a tenet of sociology, the increasing popularity of which, and its elevation to a science, attest to the hold that collectivism has on our times. The scientist is no longer honored as a bold adventurer into the unknown, in search of nature's principles, but has become a servant of Society, to which he owes his training and his keep. Heroes and heroic exploits are being demoted to accidental outcroppings of mass thought and movements. The superior person, the self-starting "captain of industry," the inherent genius—these are fictions; all are but robots made by Society.

Economics is the study of how Society makes a living, under its own techniques and prescriptions, not how individuals, in pursuit of happiness, go about the making of a living. And philosophy, or what goes by that name, has made truth itself an attribute of Society.

Collectivism is more than an idea. In itself, an idea is nothing but a toy of speculation, a mental idol. Since, as the myth holds, the suprapersonal Society is replete with possibilities, the profitable thing to do is to put the myth to work, to energize its virtue. The instrument at hand is the State, throbbing with political energy and quite willing to expend it on this glorious adventure. Thus comes Statism, or the worship of political power.

Statism is not a modern religion. Even before Plato, political philosophy concerned itself with the nature, origin, and justification of the State. But, while the thinkers speculated on it, the general public accepted political authority as a fact to be lived with and let it go at that. It is only within recent times (except, perhaps, during periods when Church and State were one, thus endowing political coercion with divine sanction) that the mass of people have consciously or implicitly accepted the Hegelian dictum that "the State is the general substance, whereof individuals are but the accidents." It is this acceptance of the State as "substance," as a suprapersonal reality, and its investment with a competence no individual can lay claim to, that is the special characteristic of the twentieth century.

In times past, the disposition was to look upon the State as something one had to reckon with, but as a complete outsider. One got along with the State as best one could, feared or admired it, hoped to be taken in by it and to enjoy its perquisites, or held it at arm's length as an untouchable thing; one hardly thought of the State as the integral of Society. One had to support the State—there was no way of avoiding taxes—and one tolerated its interventions as interventions, not as the warp and woof of life. And the State itself was proud of its position apart from, and above, Society.

The present disposition is to liquidate any distinction between State and Society, conceptually or institutionally. The State *is* Society; the social order is indeed an appendage of the political establishment, depending on it for sustenance, health, education, communications, and all things coming under the head of "the pursuit of happiness." In theory, taking college textbooks on economics and political science for authority, the integration is about as complete as words can make it. In the operation of human affairs, despite the fact that lip service is rendered the concept of inherent personal rights, the tendency to call upon the State for the solution of all the problems of life shows how far we have abandoned the doctrine of rights, with its correlative of self-reliance, and have accepted the State as the reality of Society. It is this actual integration, rather than the theory, that marks off the twentieth century from its predecessors.

One indication of how far the integration has gone is the disappearance of any discussion of the State *qua* State—a discussion that engaged the best minds of the eighteenth and nineteenth centuries. The inadequacies of a particular regime, or its personnel, are under constant attack, but there is no faultfinding with the institution itself. The State is all right, by common agreement, and it would work perfectly if the "right" people were at its helm. It does not occur to most critics of the New Deal that all its deficiencies are inherent in *any* State, under *anybody's* guidance, or that when the political establishment garners enough power a demagogue will sprout. The idea that this power apparatus is indeed the enemy of Society, that the interests of these institutions are in opposition, is simply unthinkable. If it is brought up, it is dismissed as "old-fashioned," which it is; until the modern era, it was an axiom that the State bears constant watching, that pernicious proclivities are built into it.

A few illustrations of the temper of our times come to mind.

The oft-used statement that "we owe it to ourselves," in relation to the debts incurred in the name of the State, is indicative of the tendency to obliterate from our consciousness the line of demarcation between governed and governors. It is not only a stock phrase in economics textbooks but is tacitly accepted in financial circles as sound in principle. To modern bankers, a government bond is at least as sound as an obligation of a private citizen, since the bond is in fact an obligation of the citizen to pay taxes. No distinction is made between a debt backed by production or productive ability and a debt secured by political power; in the final analysis a government bond is a lien on production, so what's the difference? By such reasoning, the interests of the public, which are always centered in the production of goods, are equated with the predatory interests of the State.

In many economics textbooks, government borrowing from citizens, whether done openly or by pressure brought upon the banks to lend their depositors' savings, is explained as a transaction equivalent to the transfer of money from one pocket to another, of the *same pants;* the citizen lends to himself what he lends to the government. The rationale of this absurdity is that the effect on the nation's economy is the same whether the citizen spends his money or the government does it for him. He has simply given up his negligible right of choice. The fact that he has no desire for what the government spends his money on, that he would not of his own free will contribute to the buying of it, is blithely over-looked.

The "same pants" notion rests on the identification of the amorphous "national economy" with the well-being of the individual; he is thus merged into the mass and loses his personality.

Of a piece with this kind of thinking is a companion phrase, "We are the government." Its use and acceptance is most illustrative of the hold collectivism has taken on the American mind in this century, to the exclusion of the basic American tradition. When the Union was founded, the overriding fear of Americans was that the new government might become a threat to their freedom, and the framers of the Constitution were hard put to allay this fear. Now it is held that freedom is a gift from government in return for subservience. The reversal has been accomplished by a neat trick in semantics. The word "democracy" is the key to this trick. When one looks for a definition of this word, one finds that it is not a form of government but rather the rule by "social attitudes." But what is a "social attitude"? Putting aside the wordy explanations of this slippery concept, it turns out to be in practice good old majoritarianism; what 51 per cent of the people deem right is right, and the minority is perforce wrong. It is the General Will fiction under a new name. There is no place in this concept for the doctrine of inherent rights; the only right left to the minority, particularly the minority of one, is conformity with the dominant "social attitude."

If "we are the government," then it follows that the man who finds himself in jail must blame himself for putting himself there, and the man who takes all the tax deductions the law allows is really cheating himself. While this may seem to be a farfetched *reductio ad absurdum*, the fact is that many an armed-services conscript consoles himself with that kind of logic. This country was largely populated by escapees from conscription—called "czarism" a generation or two ago and held to be the lowest form of involuntary servitude. Now it has come to pass that a conscript army is in fact a "democratic" army, composed of men who have made adjustment with the "social attitude" of the times. So does the run-of-the-mill draftee console himself when compelled to interrupt his dream of a career. Acceptance of compulsory military service has reached the point of unconscious resignation of personality. The individual, as individual, simply does not exist; he is of the mass.

This is the fulfillment of statism. It is a state of mind that does not recognize any ego but that of the collective. For analogy, one must go to the pagan practice of human sacrifice: when the gods called for it, when the medicine man so insisted, as a condition for prospering the clan, it was incumbent on the individual to throw himself into the sacrificial fire. In point of fact, statism is a form of paganism, for it is worship of an idol, something made by man. Its base is pure dogma. Like all dogmas this one is subject to interpretations and rationales, each with its coterie of devotees. But, whether one calls oneself a Communist, Socialist, New Dealer, or just plain "democrat," one begins with the premise that the individual is of consequence only as a servant of the mass idol. Its will be done.

It is an odd circumstance of history that the questing spirit is never obliterated or completely submerged. Social and political pressures may compel the intellectually curious to put on an appearance of conformity—since one must live in one's environment—but actual conformity is impossible for a mind of that kind. It must ask "why," even of itself. And sometimes it is hardy enough to suggest an inadequacy in the prevailing pattern of thought and to speak out against it. Even in this twentieth century there are those who hold, perhaps only in the privacy of their personality, that collectivism is erroneous and mischievous and will come to no good end. There are nonconformists who reject the Hegelian notion that "the State incarnates the Divine Idea on earth." There are some who firmly maintain that only man is made in the image of God, that the State is a false idol. They are in the minority, to be sure, as they have been throughout history; they are the "remnant" to whom Isaiah is instructed to carry the message. Perhaps these will find this inquiry into the economics of Society, Government, and the State of some interest; it was written for them.

CHAPTER 1

Economics Versus Politics

IT MAY BE that wary beasts of the forest come around to accepting the hunter's trap as a necessary concomitant of foraging for food. At any rate, the presumably rational human animal has become so inured to political interventions that he cannot think of the making of a living without them; in all his economic calculations his first consideration is, what is the law in the matter? Or, more likely, how can I make use of the law to improve my lot in life? This may be described as a conditioned reflex. It hardly occurs to us that we might do better operating under our own steam, within the limits put upon us by nature, and without political restraints, controls, or subventions. It never enters our minds that these interventionary measures are placed in our path, like the trap, for purposes diametrically opposed to our search for a better living. We automatically accept them as necessary to that purpose.

And so it has come to pass that those who write about economics begin with the assumption that it is a branch of political science. Our current textbooks, almost without exception, approach the subject from a legal standpoint: how do men make a living under the prevailing laws? It follows, and some of the books admit it, that if the laws change, economics must follow suit. It is for that reason that our college curricula are loaded down with a number of courses in economics, each paying homage to the laws governing different human activities; thus we have the economics of merchandising, the economics of real-estate operations, the economics of banking, agricultural economics, and so on. That there is a science of economics which covers basic principles that operate in all our occupations, and have nothing to do with legislation, is hardly considered. From this point of view it would be appropriate, if the law sanctioned the practice, for the curricula to include a course on the economics of slavery.

Economics is not politics. One is a science, concerned with the immutable and constant laws of nature that determine the production and distribution of wealth; the other is the art of ruling. One is amoral, the other is moral. Economic laws are self-operating and carry their own sanctions, as do all natural laws, while politics deals with man-made and man-manipulated conventions. As a science, economics seeks understanding of invariable principles; politics is ephemeral, its subject matter being the day-to-day relations of associated men. Economics, like chemistry, has nothing to do with politics.

The intrusion of politics into the field of economics is simply an evidence of human ignorance or arrogance, and is as fatuous as an attempt to control the rise and fall of tides. Since the beginning of political institutions, there have been attempts to fix wages, control prices, and create capital, all resulting in failure. Such undertakings must fail because the only competence of politics is in compelling men to do what they do not want to do or to refrain from doing what they are inclined to do, and the laws of economics do not come within that scope. They are impervious to coercion. Wages and prices and capital accumulations have laws of their own, laws which are beyond the purview of the policeman.

The assumption that economics is subservient to politics stems from a logical fallacy. Since the State (the machinery of politics) can and does control human behavior, and since men are always engaged in the making of a living, in which the laws of economics operate, it seems to follow that in controlling men the State can also bend these laws to its will. The reasoning is erroneous because it overlooks consequences. It is an invariable principle that men labor in order to satisfy their desires, or that the motive power of production is the prospect of consumption; in fact, a thing is not produced until it reaches the consumer. Hence, when the State intervenes in the economy, which it always does by way of confiscation, it hinders consumption and therefore production. The output of the producer is in proportion to his intake. It is not wilfulness that brings about this result; it is the working of an immutable natural law. The slave does not consciously "lay down on the job"; he is a poor producer because he is a poor consumer.

The evidence is that economics influences the character of politics, rather than the other way around. A communist State (which undertakes to disregard the laws of economics, as if they did not exist) is characterized by its preoccupation with force; it is a fear State. The aristocratic Greek city-State took its shape from the institution of slavery. In the nineteenth century, when the State, for purposes of its own, entered into partnership with the rising industrial class, we had the mercantilist or merchant State. The Welfare State is in fact an oligarchy of bureaucrats who, in return for the perquisites and prestige of office, undertake to confiscate and redistribute production according to formulae of their own imagination, with utter disregard of the principle that production must fall in the amount of the confiscation. It is interesting to note that all welfarism starts with a program of distribution—control of the market place with its price technique—and ends up with attempts to manage production; that is because, contrary to their expectations, the laws of economics are not suspended by their political interference, prices do not respond to their dicta, and in an effort to make their preconceived notions work they apply themselves to production, and there too they fail.

The imperviousness of economic law to political law is shown in this historic fact: in the long run every State collapses, frequently disappears altogether and becomes an archeological curio. Every collapse of which we have sufficient evidence was preceded by the same course of events. The State, in its insatiable lust for power, increasingly intensified its encroachments on the economy of the nation, causing a consequent decline of interest in production, until at long last the subsistence level was reached and not enough above that was produced to maintain the State in the condition to which it had been accustomed. It was not economically able to meet the strain of some immediate circumstance, like war, and succumbed. Preceding that event, the economy of Society, on which State power rests, had deteriorated, and with that deterioration came a letdown in moral and cultural values; men "did not care." That is, Society collapsed and drew the State down with it. There is no way for the State to avoid this consequence—except, of course, to abandon its interventions in the economic life of the people it controls, which its inherent avarice for power will not let it do. There is no way for politics to protect itself from politics.

The story of the American State is instructive. Its birth was most auspicious, being midwifed by a coterie of men unusually wise in the history of political institutions and committed to the safeguarding of the infant from the mistakes of its predecessors. Apparently, none of the blemishes of tradition marked the new State. It was not burdened with the inheritance of a feudal or a caste system. It did not have to live down the doctrine of "divine right," nor was it marked with the scars of conquest that had made the childhood of other States difficult. It was fed on strong stuff: Rousseau's doctrine that government derived its powers from the consent of the governed, Voltaire's freedom of speech and thought, Locke's justification of revolution, and, above all, the doctrine of inherent rights. There was no regime of status to stunt its growth. In fact, everything was *de novo*.

Every precautionary measure known to political science was taken to prevent the new American State from acquiring the self-destructive habit of every State known to history, that of interfering with man's pursuit of happiness. The people were to be left alone, to work out their individual destinies with whatever capacities nature had endowed them. Toward that end, the State was surrounded with a number of ingenious prohibitions and limitations. Not only were its functions clearly defined, but any inclination to go beyond bounds was presumably restrained by a tripartite division of authority, while most of the interventionary powers which the State employs were reserved for the authorities closer to the governed and therefore more amenable to their will; by the divisive principle of *imperium in imperio it* was forever, presumably, deprived of the monopoly position necessary to a State on the rampage. Better yet, it was condemned to get along on a meager purse; its powers of taxation were neatly circumscribed. It did not seem possible, in 1789, for the American State to do much in the way of interfering with the economy of the nation; it was constitutionally weak and off balance.

The ink was hardly dry on the Constitution before its authors, now in position of authority, began to rewrite it by interpretation, to the end that its bonds would loosen. The yeast of power that is imbedded in the State was in fermentation. The process of judicial interpretation, continued to the present day, was later supplemented by amendment; the effect of nearly all the amendments, since the first ten (which were written into the Constitution by social pressure), was to weaken the position of the several state governments and to extend the power of the central government. Since State power can grow only at the expense of social power, the centralization which has been going on since 1789 has pushed American Society into that condition of subservience which the Constitution was intended to prevent.

In 1913 came the amendment that completely unshackled the American State, for with the revenues derived from unlimited income taxation it could henceforth make unlimited forays into the economy of the people. The Sixteenth Amendment not only violated the right of the individual to the product of his efforts, the essential ingredient of freedom, but it also gave the American State the means to become the nation's biggest consumer, employer, banker, manufacturer, and owner of capital. There is now no phase of economic life in which the State is not a factor, there is no enterprise or occupation free of its intervention.

The metamorphosis of the American State from an apparently harmless establishment to an interventionary machine as powerful as that of Rome at its height took place within a century and a half; the historians estimate that the gestation of the greatest State of antiquity covered four centuries; we travel faster these days. When the grandeur of Rome was at its grandest, the principal preoccupation of the State was the confiscation of the wealth produced by its citizens and subjects; the confiscation was legally formalized, as it is today, and even though it was not sugar-coated with moralisms or ideologically rationalized, some features of modern welfarism were put into practice. Rome had its make-work programs, its gratuities to the unemployed, and its subsidies to industry. These things are necessary to make confiscation palatable and possible.

To the Romans of the times, this order of things probably seemed as normal and proper as it does today. The living are condemned to live in the present, under the prevailing conditions, and their preoccupation with those conditions makes any assessment of the historic trend both difficult and academic. The Romans hardly knew or cared about the "decline" in which they were living and certainly did not worry about the "fall" to which their world was riding. It is only from the vantage point of history, when it is possible to sift the evidence and find a cause-and-effect relationship, that a meaningful estimate of what was happening can be made. We know now that despite the arrogance of the State the economic forces that bear upon social trends were on the job. The production of wealth, the things men live by, declined in proportion to the State's exactions and interferences; the general concern with mere existence submerged any latent interest in cultural and moral values, and the character of Society gradually changed to that of a herd. The mills of the gods grind slow but sure; within a couple of centuries the deterioration of Roman Society was followed by the disintegration of the State, so that it had neither the means nor the will to withstand the winds of historic chance. It should be noted that Society, which flourishes only under a condition of freedom, collapsed first; there was no disposition to resist the invading hordes.

The analogy suggests a prophecy and a jeremiad. But that is not within the scope of this essay, the hypothesis of which is that Society, Government, and the State are basically economic phenomena, that a profitable understanding of these institutions will be found in economics, not in politics. This is not to say that economics can explain all the facets of these institutions, any more than the study of his anatomy will reveal all the secrets of the human being; but, as there cannot be a human being without a skeleton, so any inquiry into the mechanism of social integrations cannot bypass economic law.

For reasons that will become apparent as we go along, it is necessary to digress from the main line of thought for one chapter, which will be devoted to an examination of two theories as to the origin of the State, one being the classical theory, the other being of more recent date.

CHAPTER 2

From God or the Sword?

IS THE STATE ordered in the nature of things? The classical theorists in political science were so persuaded. Observing that every agglomeration of humans known to history was attended with a political institution of some kind, and convinced that in all human affairs the hand of God played a part, they concluded that the political organization of men enjoyed divine sanction. They had a syllogism to support their assumption: God made man; man made the State; therefore, God made the State. The State acquired divinity vicariously. The reasoning was bolstered by an analogy; it is a certainty that the family organization, with its head, is in the natural order of things, and it follows that a group of families, with the State acting as over-all father, is likewise a natural phenomenon. If deficiencies in the family occur, it is because of the ignorance or wickedness of the father; and if the social order suffers distress or disharmony it is because the State has lost sight of the ways of God. In either case, the *pater familias* needs instruction in moral principles. That is, the State, which is inevitable and necessary, might be improved upon but cannot be abolished.

Accepting *a priori* the naturalness of the State, they sought for the taproot of the institution in the nature of man. Surely, the State appears only when men get together, and that fact would indicate that its origin is lodged in the complexity of the human being; animals have no State. This line of inquiry led to contradictions and uncertainties, as it had to because the evidence as to man's nature lies in his moral behavior and this is far from uniform. Two men will respond differently to the same exigency, and even one man will not follow a constant pattern of behavior under all circumstances. The problem which the political scientists with the theological turn of mind set for themselves was to find out whether the State owed its origin to the fact that man is inherently "good" or "bad," and on this point there is no positive evidence. Hence the contradictions in their findings.

The three thinkers along these lines with whom we are most familiar, although they had their forerunners, are Thomas Hobbes, John Locke, and Jean Jacques Rousseau. As a starting point for their speculations, the three of them made use of the same hypothesis, that there was a time when men were not politically organized and lived under conditions called a "state of nature." It was pure assumption, of course, since if men ever roamed the face of the earth as thoroughgoing isolationists, having no contact with one another except at the end of a club, they never would have left any evidence of it. There must always have been at least a family organization or we would not be here to talk about a "state of nature."

At any rate, Hobbes maintained that in this pre-political state man was "brutish" and "nasty," ever poised at the property and person of his neighbor. His predatory inclination was motivated by an overweening passion for material plenty. But, says Hobbes, man was from the beginning endowed with the gift of reason, and at some point in his "natural" state his reason told him that he could do better for himself by cooperating with his fellow "natural" man. At that point he entered into a "social contract" with him, by the terms of which each agreed to abide by an authority that would restrain him from doing what his "nature" inclined him to do. Thus came the State.

Locke, on the other hand, is rather neutral in his moral findings; to him the question of whether man is "good" or "bad" is secondary to the fact that he is a creature of reason and desire. In fact, says Locke, even when he lived in his "natural" state, man's principal concern was his property, the fruit of his labor. His reason told him that he would be more secure in the possession and enjoyment of it if he submitted himself to a protective agency. He therefore entered into a "social contract" and organized the State. Locke makes the first business of the State the protection of property and asserts that when a particular State is derelict in that duty it is morally correct for the people to replace it, even by force, with another.

Looking into the "state of nature," Rousseau finds it to be an idyllic Eden, in which man was perfectly free and therefore morally perfect. There was only one flaw in this otherwise good life: the making of a living was difficult. It was to overcome the hardships of "natural" existence that he gave up some of his freedom and accepted the "social contract." As to the character of the contract, it is a blending of the will of each individual with that of every other signatory into what Rousseau calls the General Will.

Thus, while the three speculators were in some disagreement as to the nature of man, where the seed of the State was to be found, they nevertheless agreed that the State flowered from it. It should be pointed out that this attempt to find an origin of the State was not their prime purpose, that each of them was interested in a political system of his own, and that each deemed it necessary to establish an origin that would fit in with his system. It would not serve our present purpose to discuss their political philosophies, but it is interesting to note that each was fashioned to fit the exigencies of the times, giving rise to the suspicion that their theories as to origin were similarly influenced. Their common prepossession was that the State is in the natural order of things, and Hobbes gives it divine sanction. In that respect they followed tradition; early Christian speculation on the State referred to its ideal as the "City of God," and Plato spoke of his State as something "of which a pattern is made in heaven."

Modern political science passes up the question of origin, accepts the State as a going concern, makes recommendations for its operational improvement. The metaphysicians of old laid the deficiencies of a particular State to ignorance or disobedience of the laws of God. The moderns also have their ideal, or each political scientist has his own, and each has his prescription for achieving it; the ingredients of the prescription are a series of laws plus an enforcement machinery. The function of the State, it is generally assumed, is to bring about the Good Society—there being no question as to its ability to do so—and the Good Society is whatever the political scientist has in mind.

In recent times a few investigators have turned to history for evidence as to the origin of the State and have evolved what is sometimes called the theory of the sociological State.

The records show, they observe, that all primitive peoples made their living in one of two ways, agriculture or livestock raising; hunting and fishing seem to have been side lines in both economies. The requirements of these two occupations developed clearly defined and different habits and skills. The business of roaming around in search of grazing land and water called for a well-knit organization of venturesome men, while the fixed routine of farming needed no organization and little enterprise. The phlegmatic docility of scattered land workers made them easy prey for the daring herdsmen of the hills. Covetousness suggested attack.

At first, the historians report, the object of pilferage was women, since incest was tabu long before the scientists found reason to condemn the practice. The stealing of women was followed by the stealing of portable goods, and both jobs were accompanied by the wholesale slaughter of males and unwanted females. Somewhere along the line the marauders hit upon the economic fact that dead men produce nothing, and from that observation came the institution of slavery; the herdsmen improved their business by taking along captives and assigning menial chores to them. This master-slave economy, the theory holds, is the earliest manifestation of the State. Thus, the premise of the State is the exploitation of producers by the use of power.

Eventually, hit-and-run pilferage was replaced by the idea of security—or the continuing exaction of tribute from people held in bondage. Sometimes the investing tribe would take charge of a trading center and place levies on transactions, sometimes they would take control of the highways and waterways leading to the villages and collect tolls from caravans and merchants. At any rate, they soon learned that loot is part of production and that it is plentiful when production is plentiful; to encourage production, therefore, they undertook to patrol it and to maintain "law and order." They not only policed the conquered people but also protected them from other marauding tribes; in fact, it was not uncommon for a harassed community to invite a warlike tribe to come in and stand guard, for a price. Conquerors came not only from the hills, for there were also "herdsmen of the sea," tribes whose hazardous occupation made them particularly daring on the attack.

The investing people held themselves aloof from the conquered, enjoying what later became known as extraterritoriality. They maintained cultural and political ties with their homeland, they retained their own language, religion, and customs, and in most cases did not disturb the *mores* of their subjects as long as tribute was forthcoming. In time, for such is the way of propinquity, the ideational barriers between conquered and conquerors melted away and a process of amalgamation set in. The process was sometimes hastened by a severing of the ties with the homeland, as when the local chieftain felt strong enough in his new environment to challenge his overlord and to cease dividing the loot with him, or when successful insurrection at home cut him off from it. Closer contact with the conquered resulted in a blending of languages, religions, and customs. Even though intermarriage was frowned upon, for economic and social reasons, sexual attraction could not be put off by dictum, and a new generation, often smeared with the bar sinister, bridged the chasm with blood ties. Military ventures, as in defense of the now common homeland, helped the amalgam.

The blending of the two cultures gave rise to a new one, not the least important feature of which was a set of customs and laws regularizing the accommodation of the dues-paying class to their masters. Necessarily, these conventions were formulated by the latter, with the intent of freezing their economic advantage into a legacy for their offspring. The dominated people, who at first had resisted the exactions, had long ago been worn out by the unequal struggle and had resigned themselves to a system of taxes, rents, tolls, and other forms of tribute. This adjustment was facilitated by the inclusion of some of the "lower classes" into the scheme, as foremen, bailiffs, and menial servitors, and military service under the masters made for mutual admiration if not respect. Also, the codifying of the exactions eventually obliterated from memory the arbitrariness with which they had been introduced and covered them with an aura of correctness. The laws fixed limits on the exactions, made excesses irregular and punishable, and thus established "rights" for the exploited class. The exploiters wisely guarded these "rights" against trespass by their own more avaricious members, while the exploited, having made a comfortable adjustment to the system of exactions, from which some of them often profited, achieved a sense of security and self-esteem in this doctrine of "rights." Thus, through psychological and legal processes that stratification of Society became fixed. The State is that class which enjoys economic preference through its control of the machinery of enforcement.*

The sociological theory of the State rests not only on the evidence of history but also on the fact that there are two ways by which men can acquire economic goods : production and predation. The first involves the application of labor to raw materials, the other the use of force. Pillaging, slavery, and conquest are the primitive forms of predation, but the economic effect is the same when political coercion is used to deprive the producer of his product, or even when he accedes to the transfer of ownership as the price for permission to live. Nor is predation changed to something else when it is done in the name of charity—the Robin Hood formula. In any case, one enjoys what another has produced, and to the extent of the predation the producer's desires must go unsatisfied, his labor unrequited. It will be seen that in its moral aspect the sociological theory leans on the doctrine of private property, the inalienable right of the individual to the product of his effort, and holds that any kind of coercion, exercised for any purpose whatsoever, does not alienate that right. We shall take up that point later.

Incidentally, at first glance this theory seems to bear a resemblance to the dictum of Karl Marx that the State is the managing committee for the capitalistic class. But the resemblance is in the words, not in the ideas. The Marxian theory maintains that the State in other hands—the "dictatorship of the proletariat"—could abolish exploitation. But the sociological theory of the State (or the conquest theory) insists that the State itself, regardless of its composition, is an exploitative institution and cannot be anything else; whether it takes over the property of the owner of wages or the property of the owner of capital, the ethical principle is the same. If the State takes from the capitalist to give to the worker, or from the mechanic to give to the farmer, or from all to better itself, force has

24

been used to deprive someone of his rightful property, and in that respect it is carrying on in the spirit, if not the manner, of original conquest.

Therefore, if the chronology of any given State does not begin with conquest, it nevertheless follows the same pattern because its institutions and practices continue in the tradition of those States that have gone through the historic process. The American State did not begin with conquest; the Indians had no property that could be lifted and, being hunters by profession, they were too intractable to be enslaved. But the colonists were themselves the product of an exploitative economy, had become inured to it in their respective homelands, had imported and incorporated it in their new organization. Many of them came to their new land bearing the yoke of bondage. All had come from institutional environments that had emerged from conquest; they knew nothing else, and when they set up institutions of their own they simply transplanted these environments. They brought the predatory State with them.

Any profitable inquiry into the character of the American State must therefore take into account the distinction between making a living by production and gaining a living by predation; that is, between economics and politics.

* This brief summary of the historical background of the sociological theory suggests Old Testament stories of the conquest of Canaan by the Israelites, the history of England and of the Roman Empire. However, the principal proponents of this theory, Gumplowicz and Oppenheimer, were more interested in the origin of the State than in its development, and they dug into the records of early tribes all over the world; wherever they looked they found that the political organization began with conquest.

CHAPTER 3

The Unit of Social Life

BEGINNING WITH THE OBVIOUS—there must be men before there is a Society, and there must be a Society before there is a Government. Social institutions must seminate in the soil of which the individual is made. Therefore, we are compelled to ask the individual, the unit of social life, to tell us why he socializes, why he becomes political. The metaphysicians were on the right track when they inquired into the nature of the individual for an explanation of the State, even though they were sidetracked by their theological turn of mind. That way lies no positive answer, nor one that does not begin with making assumptions. Perhaps a surer light on the question will be thrown if we look at the human being externally, without reference to his spiritual composition.

What do we observe as a constant in his career? To that question there is but one answer: that he is always, and wherever we find him, concerned with making a living. We cannot even think of a human being who is rid of that preoccupation. He is, basically, an "economic man"—to use a term that is sometimes used derogatorily, but which is most appropriate when we reflect that man's primordial business is existence. His economic pursuit is ingrained in him as a matter of necessity. It seems logical to assume, then, that the Society in which we always find him is either a phase of, or is related to, the business from which he never retires. Is it not likely that if we apply ourselves to the means and methods he employs in the gaining of a living we shall learn that Society and Government are outgrowths of that process? Perhaps, after all, these institutions have their roots in economics. It is a plausible hypothesis at any rate.

The objection has been raised that the human being is far too complex to be treated only as a living creature. Other species that inhabit the earth are also on the constant prowl for the means of existence and they do not have anything like what we call Society and Government; the best they do in the way of socializing is a herd or a school or a flock, which are entirely different organizations from those which are formalized. This objection, however, stems from that limited and unreal definition of "economic man" which describes his life purpose as the mere acquisition of food, raiment, and shelter. Such a man does not exist, or exists only under the compulsion of necessity. To man, unlike other living creatures, the "making of a living" only begins with providing the necessaries, for he is so constituted that once that problem is solved, or even before it is fully solved, his imagination gives rise to other desires which, when gratified, give rise to still other desires and so on *ad infinitum*. His job of 'living" has no fixed perimeter. Yet, the satisfaction of every desire that springs from his fancy involves the same means and methods that he employs in securing the necessaries. The book and the violin come into being by processes that are in essence the same as those applied to the making of bread and clothes; everything man wants involves the machinery of production. Hence, the "economic man" is not a special kind of man, and though for purposes of study we may in our mental laboratory segregate him from the "cultural man," the "religious man," or the "military man," he is in fact only man utilizing economic means in pursuit of whatever "living" his inclination or chance leads him to. The catalytic agent of all human aspirations is production.

What, then, is production? It is the application of labor to the raw materials that nature provides for the making of things that satisfy human desires. Nothing can be produced in any other way. True, there are things men want that apparently do not involve the use of raw materials, things that are usually described as services. But even the singer needs sustenance, and the naked preacher might find the cold a hindrance to thought. There is no desirable service so far removed from basic production—like insurance or education—but that upon examination it does not turn out to be a subdivision or offshoot of the application of labor to raw materials. When you think of it, you realize that all the tangibles that men desire, like food and raiment, are congealed services, like cooking and designing, and therefore any distinction between goods and services, in an economic sense, is academic.

The fact that man is invariably dependent on raw materials for his living, even in the widest sense of living, stamps him as a "land animal." But, in that respect, every other animal is similarly circumscribed. So, the question arises, in what respect does the human being, whose social institutions concern us, differ from his food-grubbing neighbors? It is in the fact that he is not, like them, dependent on what he finds, but has the capacity of making use of nature to further his ends. This capacity we call reason, which is the faculty of extracting from a number of related phenomena a causative principle and of applying this principle in his business. For instance, he observes that nature does not grow edible things just anywhere and at any time, but only when and where soil of a given texture enjoys a given amount of sunshine and a given amount of moisture.

Learning these secrets of nature, he sets them down in formulae, which he calls natural laws. Then, guiding himself by these laws, he goes about growing the food he wants; he becomes a maker of abundance. That, his animal friends cannot do.

We say man "conquers" nature, but the fact is his conquest consists of accommodating himself to the means employed by nature in achieving its ends; he cannot get the results he is after unless he learns and makes himself subservient to its laws. Primitive people are primitive simply because they have not gotten around to fathoming these laws and making use of them. And the failures of what we call the "civilized" man, in whatever field he chooses to operate, are likewise due to his ignorance of nature's laws or his arrogance in trying to make his way in disregard of them; they are, however, immutable and self-enforcing, and his failures indicate that they carry their own sanctions. He builds an atomic bomb because he has mastered the physical laws pertaining thereto; he destroys Society with it because he neither knows nor is willing to submit to the social laws that nature has writ in its book of knowledge. He is particularly at a disadvantage when he declares (as he sometimes does, especially in the fields of economics and social science) that there are no natural laws, that man is uninhibited by any such fictions; that's when he gets himself into real trouble.

Given the natural resources and a knowledge of nature's laws, the making of a living calls for an expenditure of labor. That is the inexorable price of production. But the expenditure of labor induces the unpleasant experience of weariness, something man does not want. (We are concerned only with labor expended for economic purposes. Sometimes man will find pleasure in exertion itself, as in taking a walk. And sometimes he "likes his job," finds enjoyment in the doing, regardless of any other returns. The exhilaration resulting from the doing is the profit he seeks. But he does not labor for the sake of laboring.) To avoid exertion, man might, like other animals, curtail his appetites to the barest necessities, to the things that make existence possible and that can be had with the minimum of effort. (Nothing can be had with no effort.) He is, however, not so constituted, being driven by an ever-expanding curiosity to seek new gratifications, and he is ever looking to nature to tell him how he can acquire them with less labor. He invents labor-saving devices; he expends labor to save labor. He puts in "overtime"—or labor in excess of what is necessary to keep him alive—in the production of things that will save him labor in his future enterprises or will enable him to better his circumstances. We call those things capital. As far as we know, man has always been a capitalist, a storer up of labor, and we cannot conceive of a time when he was not making such tools. Thus, the stone axe which he made to subdue an edible beast became, after centuries of reflection and trial-and-error, a cleaving knife and the Chicago stockyards. Capital accumulation has always been man's career. We do not know of a noncapitalistic man or a noncapitalistic Society. In any distinction between primitive man and civilized man we use as a yardstick their relative accumulations and use of capital.

A natural law is derived from observation of the ways of nature. Its first characteristic is invariability—it always happens that way; there are no exceptions. And since, in everything he does, as far back as we have any knowledge of him, so that we cannot even conceive of a deviation, *man seeks to satisfy his desires with the least expenditure of labor*, we can put that down as a natural law of human behavior. A second requirement of a natural law is that it enables us to predict what will happen in the future, and the rule above qualifies on that score. We invent and make household appliances because we know that every housewife is interested in saving labor; we offer bribes to officials because we are ever on the lookout for "something for nothing," and if the officials accept the bribes it is because they prefer to get their satisfactions without an expenditure of labor. Our entire price structure is based on that "law of parsimony." In fact, every economic theory must take it into account, and social doctrines that leave it out of consideration prove impracticable; when, for instance, it is proposed that men sell their products for less than the cost of production, or for less than other men are willing to pay for them, we have what is called a "black market." Our immediate reaction to the socialistic notion that men will put out labor with abandon and with little regard for returns is that it is nonsensical; humans don't act that way.

Now, Society, Government, and the State are institutions that men make, and it must be taken for granted that these too are expressions of this law of human behavior. If in all his other undertakings he is invariably motivated by this aversion to labor, why should we assume that it plays no part in his social and political organization? He does not undergo a mutation when he socializes and politicalizes; he is still the same man. Perhaps, after all, his institutions are, in one way or another, analogous to labor-saving devices. It makes better sense to approach an inquiry into his institutions with such a hypothesis than to begin by positing the idea that his institutions arise from forces outside of him, forces that use him as an instrument, not as the creator, as the metaphysicians and the socialists do.

Correlating with this "law of parsimony" is another constant characteristic of the human which throws light on his institutions. It is the fact that he is the only animal whose desires are never satisfied. He does not shun labor merely for the sake of shunning it; he is not lazy. In fact, we find him investing every saving of labor in a new desire, one that he was hardly aware of before he had a surplus of energy to put into it. When he masters the art of grubbing for a livelihood and finds it easy, he begins to think of tablecloths and music with his meals. His living consists of a constant climb to greater heights, to what are sometimes called luxuries or marginal satisfactions, such as books, rare stamps, baseball, and Beethoven. *Man's desires are unlimited*. But each new step in the search for a fuller life must be preceded by some shortcut in the securing of those things he has become accustomed to enjoy, and luxuries become necessities in proportion to the ease with which they can be had. Since the beginning of time, as far as we know, man has been a labor saver, a capitalist, not that he might hoard energy but that he might expend it in further accomplishment. It is for this reason, as we shall see, that Society becomes his natural habitat.

The "law of parsimony" does not maintain that men always satisfy their desires with the least exertion; it says that they *seek* to do so. Ignorance of the shortest cut, the easiest means, is the reason for his taking the longest way around. Before he knew about the automobile, the oxcart had to take care of his transportation, but as his aversion to labor caused him to invent that primitive improvement over walking, so did it spur him to the invention of the automobile; speed is an economy of effort for the accomplishment of results. The psychopath turns to stealing because he thinks that is the easiest way to satisfy his desires, and the shrewd monopolist is one who contrives to improve his circumstances without putting out the effort that competition would impose upon him. Every crime in the calendar, every social evil, every piece of political skulduggery is traceable to the "law of parsimony." So is every advance in the sciences and the arts.

It is beyond the mark to moralize about this aversion to labor *qua* labor. It is as amoral as the hair on a man's head. But if one looks into human psychology one can find there the germ of an ethical principle in this law of behavior. There it will be found that the value the individual puts on himself is measured in terms of the labor he must put out to satisfy his desires. His ego expands or contracts in proportion to the labor cost of his living. Thus, a slave, who reaps a bare existence from his exertions, makes mental adjustment to that rate of pay and acquires what we call a slave psychology; that is, he thinks of himself as not worth more than what he gets. On the other hand, the "big shot" gangster looms large in his estimation of himself because with no apparent expenditure of labor he is able to live in luxury. The self-opinion of both the slave and the "big shot" is shared by their contemporaries simply because their self-evaluation is similarly measured. The adulation we accord the opulent man and our vicarious enjoyment of cinema luxuries evidence the workings of the "law of parsimony"; it is not so much that our envy is pricked, for this only stirs us to emulation or to theft; it is that what we desire has been acquired with no visible expenditure of effort; it is the *summum bonum*. That being so, an economy so managed as to provide a general abundance, an economy of plenty, must improve the self-esteem or morale of those who enjoy it, while an economy of scarcity has the opposite effect; to put it otherwise, low prices (or easy accessibility) induce higher human values, while high prices (in terms of labor expenditure) tend to depreciate them. But that is another matter. The point is that there are moral consequences of the "law of parsimony."

Whatever other attributes the human being brings to bear on the social order of which he is the integral, his will to live comes first in the hierarchy; the will to live is not mere clinging to existence but is also an urge to improve one's circumstances and to widen one's horizon. This is innate; Nirvana, or the negation of desire, is an acquired characteristic, requiring much exercise of the will. The urge to live is accompanied by means and methods that are also built in—the inclination to avoid labor. Society may be accounted for by other human characteristics, such as man's metaphysical make-up, his cultural aspirations, and his craving for companionship. But these are debatable variables. There is no question about the persistence and universality of the attributes mentioned, and therefore they must be considered prime imperatives. However else we try to explain Society, Government, and the State, we cannot ignore the "economic man."

CHAPTER 4

Society Are People

SOCIETY IS A COLLECTIVE CONCEPT and nothing else; it is a convenience for designating a number of people. So, too, is family or crowd or gang, or any other name we give to an agglomeration of persons. Society is different from these other collective nouns in that it conveys the idea of a purpose or point of contact in which each individual, while retaining his identity and pursuing his private concerns, has an interest. A family is held together by family ties, a crowd consists of a number of people bent on some common venture, such as a baseball game or a lecture. Society, on the other hand, embraces the father and the son, the doctor and the farmer, the financier and the laborer—a host of people following all sorts of vocations and avocations, pursuing a variety of goals, each in his own way, and yet held together by a purpose which is in each of them. But Society is still a word, not an entity. It is not an extra "person"; if the census totals a hundred million, that's all there are, not one more, for there cannot be any accretion to Society except by procreation. The concept of Society as a metaphysical person falls flat when we observe that Society disappears when the component parts disperse; as in the case of a "ghost town" or of a civilization we learn about by the artifacts they left behind. When the individuals disappear so does the whole. The whole has no separate existence.

Using the collective noun with a singular verb leads us into a trap of the imagination; we are prone to personalize the collectivity and to think of it as having a body and a psyche of its own. We transfer to this mental fabrication some habits or characteristics of the individuals who are the reality; rather, we pick out of the heterogeneity some traits that seem to be common to all the parts and ascribe them to the image in our minds. And so we speak of a Mormon Society, an agricultural Society, an advanced Society; in point of fact, Society cannot be religious, has no occupation, is incapable of advancement; these are attributes of individual persons. It is a legerdemain of language. We invent a word to create an impression rather than a measurable fact, and then we use the word as if indeed it does represent a measurable fact.

All of which is self-evident and would hardly be worth mentioning if this literary usage did not lead us into blind alleys. From describing

Society as if it were a person, we slide into the habit of judging each member of the group by our impression of the whole, and of acting upon that judgment. By this mental trick the well-advertised pathology of the Nazi hierarchy was transferred to all Germans and, as its enemy, we decided that the only good German was a dead one. The mass mania of war is a product of this habit of personification; it then becomes a matter of honor, not a murder, to destroy the uniform of this personification. This negation of the individual, by use of words, is the premise of every socialistic rationale; socialism hasn't a leg to stand on until the individual, like a lump of sugar, is verbally dissolved in the personification of a class. Every political scheme to "improve" Society rests on this trick of words.

For that reason it is necessary to point out that Society is nothing but a handy word, a symbol, and that we are talking about persons, each driven by the primordial urgency to live, according to his lights and by the limitations of his inherent capacities. Society is an institution invented by man to further his purposes and his aspirations. It is, like a labor-saving device, something that helps him improve his circumstances with a saving of effort.

Everything is entitled to a beginning, and the beginning of Society has long engaged the curiosity of philosophic speculation. In that field it has become almost an axiom that Society began with the organization of the family. That may or may not be true. Yet, the theory does not explain the known organization of groups where the binding tie of consanguinity was missing, as often happened in the colonization of America or the settling of our West. If there ever was a "first" Society, it is reasonable to presume it came about just as did these communities; assuming, of course, that man is what he always was. Of the inception and development of these communities we have complete records—they happened, so to speak, under our noses—and their gestation followed a pattern so uniform as to suggest a principle of Society.

Every pioneer, alone or in family, who settled on a spot around which a metropolis eventually grew had to forage for such necessaries as nature could supply him almost ready-made. That was so whether he was an escapee from the gallows or from religious persecution. Being human, he selected for his workshop that place which, because of fertility of soil, supply of water, abundance of wild life, promised to yield him the highest wages for his labor. The job-and-home seeker in the second covered wagon is likewise influenced in his selection of a location, but as between two or more locations of equal promise he picks one nearest his predecessor. Why? The solace and comfort of companionship is a consideration. But neighborliness that is confined to passing the time of day is rather thin stuff, and will not last long unless it is implemented with a substantial binding. That binding is the increase of satisfactions made possible by cooperation, in the building of a house, in putting up a supply of kindling wood, in the quartering of an animal. In many jobs two can produce more than twice as much as each worker going it alone, while some tasks simply cannot be performed by one man. As a result of cooperative effort each has more satisfactions, more wages. Sociability thrives on the mutual profits of cooperation, and when we observe how acquaintance ripens into friendship as the mutually created wage level rises, it is hard to tell which is cause and which is effect.

Immigration to the community is in proportion to the opportunities for profitable employment afforded by this environment as against others that may be available. New workers all are lured by the prospect of self-improvement. Though they come from rack-rented Ireland or the marginal mountains of Sweden, though they speak the jargon of the ghetto or wallow in Slavic consonants, whether they escaped from the squalor of Welsh mining towns or the jobless shops of New England, they find in this selected location a common point of contact: an abundance burgeoning from nature and cooperation. Differences in race, religion, languages, and customs arouse curiosity, and sometimes irritation, but the contribution of each worker to the general fund of wealth tends to liquidate these surface dissimilarities. The rising wage level makes for a blending of cultural particularisms.

As soon as subsistence ceases to be a pressing problem, as evidenced by the bulging barn, an urgency arises for satisfactions that during the economy of scarcity were hardly dreams. The log cabin which was castle enough is now in dire need of curtains, furniture, pictures; a sense of dignity suggests a Sunday go-to-meeting suit of clothes; the barn that served as a place of worship must be supplanted with a fitting edifice; and every mother thinks of the world her son could conquer if the vistas of learning were opened for him. But the satisfaction of these new desires calls for specialized labor, for skills and knowledge which the self-sufficient jack-of-all-trades does not have. At this point in the growth of Society comes, either from within the group or from outside, one who because of his aptitude for the trade offers his services as a blacksmith. The need for such services suggests to him that the others will pay him at least as much as he can earn at the common extractive occupation. The profit motive—that is, the urge to satisfy desires with the least exertion—turns him into a specialist. But the profit motive works bilaterally. The farmer who patronizes the specialist does so because he can more profitably put in his time at farming than at blacksmithing. The relationship between buyer and seller rests on reciprocal gains.

The specialist does not appear until there is population enough to need him, and until that population has acquired an abundance. It is the stored-up labor in the barns, the capital, that suggests the possibility of hiring a tailor, a preacher, a teacher or pedlar, of getting rid of the do-it-yourself jobs which necessity forces on them, which they do as best they can and which interfere with the work they are better equipped to do. Capital accumulation is the necessary antecedent of specialization. As more and more producers come to this pioneer community, either as specialists or primary extractors (who become, by the shifting of marginal burdens to others, specialists on their own account), the capital or savings accounts swell, all the while awakening new desires. That is the way of man. In a century or two, capital accumulations reach a point where the cobbler is replaced by a shoe factory, the pedlar by a department store, and the little red schoolhouse by a college. Specialization has piled on specialization not by conscious design and certainly not by coercion, but by (a) increasing population, (b) a consequent rise in the level of wages, and (c) the savings that this rise makes possible. Trace these factors to their causative principle and you come to the workings of the "economic man"—seeking ever to improve his circumstances and to widen his circumstances by the most efficient means at his disposal.

We are speaking of the rise and development of American Society. Other social integrations, like those of Tibet or Abyssinia, never emerged from the primitive stage, and still others, like those of Europe, took a much longer time in arriving at a comparative level. The difference cannot be accounted for by the make-up of these peoples, for the American Society is a composite of the peoples of the world, each of whom played their economic part according to the script. No doubt, climatic conditions and the availability of natural resources influenced the course of American Society, for man is, after all, a "land animal." But other peoples similarly blessed did not "go places," or as fast, and for cause we must look to some special advantage the American enjoyed. By the process of elimination we come to this special advantage: freedom. Not only freedom from political restraints but also freedom from the inhibitions that institutionalized tradition imposes on man's aspirations. The early American did not have an expensive government to support, little in the way of taxation to deprive him of his savings, no traditional caste system to depress his sense of self-importance. A few of these restraining influences he did import, to his hindrance, but they had not had time enough to become entrenched and institutionalized in the wilderness. He was free to work out his destiny according to his capacities. And he chose to follow his natural bent, to better his wages by cooperation and specialization, to save some of the increase and to invest it in devices that enabled him to produce more with less effort. He was a capitalist on the loose.

Society is a growth, with roots imbedded in its component units. It is no more a manufactured thing than is a tree, although like the tree its growth can be impeded by artificial impediments or facilitated by their removal. There is a current conceit that Society can be fabricated, like a chair or a shoe, by imposing the achievements of one group of people on another. Seeing that the special characteristic of what we call an advanced culture is its fund of capital, the conceit holds that the showering of this fund on a "backward" people will speed their advancement. The idea is as silly as that of forcing a child to keep pace with an adult. A factory does not make Society, but a Society makes a factory. When an itinerant tailor could take care of their clothing needs, the pioneer community would have found a clothing factory in its midst something of a monstrosity; only when the population was large enough and productive enough to take care of its antecedent desires did the idea of a steel mill suggest itself. One gratification gives rise to another desire, and if the second calls for techniques hitherto unknown, man will take thought and invent them. But he must have freedom to do so. That is what a "backward" people lack most; either expropriation of their goods discourages production and makes accumulation impossible, or habits of mind induced by political or cultural institutions inhibit the impulse to dream. The necessary ingredient of progress is freedom.

The benefits of specialization are not without offset. As the pioneer turns more and more to the professional carpenter for help, he loses the skill which necessity forced him to develop, and the son who eventually takes over the establishment is unable to put up a shelf in the house his father built whole. The correlative of specialization is interdependence. In a highly developed Society, where each worker's contribution is a small fraction of the whole, the reliance of one on another is the condition of existence. New York hungers when a snow storm cuts off its means of communication with the farm.

It is this fact that lends credence to the fantasy of a transcendent Society. When we think of the myriad of workers involved in the production of a cup of coffee—plantation workers and bank presidents, dockmen and railroad engineers, dairy farmers and sugar refiners—we are overwhelmed by the immensity of the process and are prone to personalize it; a mental trick not unlike that of deifying the incomprehensible storm. Yet, there is no such thing as "social production"—if by that term something more than individual production is implied. Society cannot produce a thing; only individuals produce. Though a million men are involved in the job, each one, as an individual, had a hand in the production of that cup of coffee. If one of the million drops out of the line and is not replaced, the cup of coffee is not produced, does not reach the consumer. The output of the conveyor belt is in exact proportion to the number of workers who man it.

You come to the same conclusion when you answer the question, why do men work? To satisfy their desires—and for no other reason. The clerk who makes out the bill of lading for the shipment of coffee is not motivated by an interest in that document or in the coffee; he does the job only because by that means he can satisfy his desires, among which coffee may not be an item. If it were not possible for him to exchange the proceeds of his effort for the things he desires, he would have to give up clerking and address himself to the getting of those things some other way—perhaps by going back to a primitive economy. Every worker works for himself. Every worker is impelled to labor by the will to live, and there is no way of transferring that will to another person or a collectivity of persons. Therefore, the hypnotic phrase "social production"—as meaning more than the sum total of the production of individuals—is only a mischievous abstraction that bears watching. It is a phrase that looms large in the jargon of socialism.

Society consists of Tom and Dick and Harry.

CHAPTER 5

"Easy Come, Easy Go"

SHORTLY AFTER our frontiersmen settled down in their chosen workshop, one of them went fishing. His catch was far in excess of his desire for fish, and the problem of what to do with this abundance arose. His neighbor solved the problem by expressing a desire for this edible. The latter was also burdened by a plenty of something, say potatoes, of which the fisherman was in short supply. Or, maybe the grower expected a large crop of potatoes and promised the fisherman that when it was harvested some of it would be set aside for him. At any rate, an immediate or prospective exchange was decided upon, the effect of which was to enrich the menus of the exchangers. Thus, an increase of their respective satisfactions, or wages, resulted, and the seed of Main Street was sown.

There are some who maintain that Society owes its origin to the human instinct of gregariousness. But gregariousness and exchange are so closely interwoven that it is impossible to determine precedence, and when one takes into consideration that companionship is in itself a trade, though not an economic one, the distinction becomes meaningless. The market place is the soul of Society. One could not exist without the other, and both owe their origin to man's never-ending search for a fuller life. It is the market place that makes specialization possible, for it is the means by which the abundance produced by the specialist, of things that do not directly cater to his desire, is translated into things that do. And no matter how large the population grows, how varied the specializations engaged in, how intricate the technique of trade, the market place is simply the means by which one gives up what one wants less to obtain what one wants more.

What one *wants* less for what one *wants* more! Every trade, therefore, originates in desire, the desire of the seller and the desire of the buyer. Each is conscious of a greater urge for the thing offered than for the thing he must give up as a condition for possession, and when the trade is made, these purely subjective experiences find a meeting point, something we call price.* But, preceding price, preceding trade, is the human capacity of setting store on desires. It is a psychological process to which we give the name of value.

Speculation on the nature of value often takes the turn of trying to harness it in a formula of utility: how much more useful is the thing given

38

up than the thing acquired, to each party of the trade. But mathematics is incapable of measuring the elusive variable of human desire. The wealth of a nation is measured in billions; how much value does the starving citizen put on the wealth of the nation? To the owner of bonds and mortgages these papers are valuable because they enable him to satisfy his desires; but to the debtor class they represent hardship. Figures cannot express the delight of one woman who comes into possession of a washing machine, or the revulsion of a "career woman" at the thought of it. Why people want what, why their esteem of the same thing varies from time to time, why they prefer one thing to another, are questions that cannot be answered mathematically. When we look to the taproot of value we come to an enigma of life. And yet, like so many phenomena that defy analysis, value as a function is quite understandable, and as a function it explains the market place, which is the *alter ego* of Society.

The essence of value is the human capacity of measuring intensity of desire. When the two frontiersmen bartered their respective abundances, their desires were limited to the necessaries. As increasing population makes for a greater subdivision of labor, and therefore for a greater variety of goods and services, this problem of evaluating desires and of exerting one's will in favor of this or that satisfaction becomes correspondingly more intricate. When the choice lay between a bear skin and going naked, the problem of raiment was readily resolved. But now the matter involves a choice between a two-button and a three-button suit, between blue and gray, to say nothing of the quality of workmanship or correctness of size; also, population has brought a new influence to bear upon the evaluation, that of public opinion, and style becomes a consideration. Antecedent to the clothing problem, moreover, a decision must be made between clothing and a harness for the horse or a set of books for the children. The desires are many. What constriction, in the nature of things, compels a decision in favor of one gratification over another? What is the true measure of intensity of desire? The answer that man gives to this question is a ratio between variables: that gratification which, taking into consideration all the factors of inclination, environment, and necessity, will yield him the most satisfaction, according to his lights, in return for the least amount of effort that must be given up to acquire it. For it is written in the book of life that the cost of every "good" is that undesirable thing called effort.

Thus labor, in juxtaposition to desire, is the ultimate determinant of value. Let us keep in mind, however, that it is not the labor invested in producing the "good" which fixes its value—not the "cost of production"—but the labor one must give up as the price of possession.*
The fisherman was not unaware of the effort expended in getting the fish,

effort he might have put into growing potatoes, and the other frontiersman knows how much time he invested in his tubers. This awareness of labor cost bears heavily on their respective evaluations of their desires for the things offered in trade; therefore, the cost of production (or the cost of reproduction) tends to approximate the price of gratification.

It would not serve the purposes of this essay—which is concerned with the economic forces that underlie social institutions—to delve into the theory, or theories, of value, or the related subject of price. It is enough to point out that were it not for this human capacity to make evaluations there would be no market place, and if there were no market place there would be no Society. Despite all the recondite thought that has been put into this subject, no definition of value offered is quite as definitive as the popular phrase "easy come, easy go." What one acquires with little effort one has little reluctance to part with if in so doing one can obtain something wanted; on the other hand, if the getting of a pair of shoes calls for the giving up of a month's labor, an inhibitory influence comes into play and maybe the old shoes will be pressed into service for a while longer. It is this interplay of two psychological forces—intensity of desire and aversion to labor—that is the essence of value, and any attempt to reduce it to a mathematical formula is fatuous; to do so would require an understanding of the inner workings of every individual, under all circumstances, and that calls for omniscience. When a trade is consummated, the psychological forces come to rest, and this objective act is a historical fact that is measurable; that is, the price agreed upon tells us something about what the buyer and seller had been cogitating upon before the trade took place. There is no way of measuring their antecedent emotional experiences. And even then, even after the trade has been consummated, it cannot be said with certainty that it will be repeated. The determination of value in the future is largely guesswork. That is why there are "mark down" sales.

This impossibility of fixing future values is the rock on which "economic planning" founders. Not only is the planner without data on which to base his prognoses, but the plannee himself cannot furnish it. No man can foretell with certainty what he will want at a future time, or how much he will want it, for no man can predict the influences that will determine his decisions. Today he is most anxious to have a hat, but tomorrow he is convinced that headgear causes loss of hair and he decides to go uncovered; or the repair of his roof is a more pressing need than the automobile he had set his heart on; or a lessening of his income compels a reevaluation of his desires. Variability of choice makes predictions most precarious, as producers well know. The best the planner can do is to forecast "average" desires on the basis of past experience. But the "average" necessarily eliminates the desires of last years minority, who may be the majority this year.

Confronted with this problem of variability in desires, the "economic planner" must resort to constriction, to limitation of choice, to the strangulation of imagination. The planner undertakes to prescribe what the individual *should* want, and the basis for his prescription is a conviction that he knows best what is "good" for the individual. Because it is in the market place that variability of choice expresses itself, through price, the planner's conceit leads him to attempt to control consumption by controlling price. But price is not controllable, simply because desires are not controllable. The barrier to free choice which the planner sets up acts like the dam in the river; the water does not stop flowing but either overflows the dam or spreads out in a lake. Price control does not stop wanting or bidding; it simply creates what propaganda calls a "black market," which is in fact the true market, somewhat distorted but nevertheless true. It may be illegal but it is highly moral, for it arises from the individual's right to himself, to the product of his labors, and to the pursuit of happiness which is the essence of living.

Since the control of consumption by means of fixed prices proves impossible, the planner turns to constricting productive specialization. That is, he undertakes to desocialize Society. As we have seen, men come together and cooperate for the improvement of their circumstances—to raise their common wage level—and they accomplish this purpose through specialization; any attempt to constrict specialization is therefore unnatural and regressive; to the extent that if it succeeds it tends to break up the integration or to retard its growth. Men must then get along on less. But it is not in the nature of men to get along on less, and to counteract this inner drive the planner must resort to violence. All "economic planning" ultimately rests on purging. Purging of what? Of the impulses on which Society is built. The "economic planner" does not control prices or production; he polices men.

Value is a deeply human experience, and it is individual. There is no way for the individual to transfer his value concepts to another; there is no way of collectivizing value. It is a ratio between intensity of desire and aversion to labor and can be compared to a measuring stick on which is recorded the esteem that man puts on the energy stored up in him. It is the economic phrasing of his self-worth. When a great supply of the things he lives by reduces the amount of labor he must give up to get them, his worth to himself is enhanced; for the energy thus saved becomes investable in a further improvement of his circumstances. His horizon expands. He thinks of Beethoven and baseball because of the ease with which his primary desires can be satisfied. A general abundance, therefore, is synonymous with both low prices and a wider scope for life. Contrariwise, the high prices brought about by a scarcity of goods signify that more energy has to be expended to satisfy one's needs, that the worth of human effort has declined. The cheaper things are, the richer man is.*

It is, then, by production, by abundance that man lifts his wage level and his self-worth. His pursuit of happiness is favored by the ease with which he can acquire satisfactions, and is hindered by the difficulties that nature or man-made institutions may interpose. Among the labor-saving devices that facilitate the exchange of abundances arising from specialization is money. Money is a token that something of a given value has been produced and, by custom and common consent, is accepted as a claim on production of comparable value. It is a commodity that, in the area in which its value is generally recognized, is exchangeable for all other commodities, thus obviating burdensome barter. But it is itself of no value, except as metal or paper, and is esteemed only because it is accepted in the market place as an evidence that goods or services have been made available, that the general abundance has been increased by labor. In the final analysis, money is a receipt for services performed; for that reason it achieves importance as a measurement of value. However, the yardstick is not and cannot be made a substitute for the goods measured, and money is not production.

The wide acceptance of the measurement of value suggests to the "economic planner" that he can control consumption and regulate production by tinkering with this accepted yardstick. By surreptitiously changing the standard from thirty-six to thirty-three inches, he induces the buyer into believing that he has acquired more goods. But no more goods has been produced by this trick, and the buyer finds that the cloth he purchased is not enough for the suit of clothes he expected to get out of the yardage. He has been cheated. As a result of this experience, his esteem of money drops; he demands more of it in exchange for his labor. And that is all that the "economic planner" has accomplished; he neither controls consumption nor regulates production by his counterfeit operation. Until his trickery is discovered, Society has been robbed of some of its output; but the robbery, when discovered, undermines confidence in the market place, discourages production (and therefore consumption), until Society insists on the correction of the wrong done it. The net effect of inflation, of cheapening the value of money, is to retard mans pursuit of happiness.

To sum up, it is the human capacity for evaluating desires and making choices that is the motive power of Society. Were it not for this phenomenon the market place would never arise and the abundance of specialization would be impossible. And man would be reduced to grubbing along on what he would find in nature, like other animals. No other animal gives evidence of a consciousness of comparable desires. No other animal shows a capacity of measuring one want against another or of acting upon a decision resulting from such comparison; that is, of deliberately relinquishing possession of one desirable thing for the purpose of acquiring another. No other animal trades. On the other hand, this potential pervades man's existence; he could hardly exist without a sense of value. From cradle to grave, man is ever making distinctions in desirability. Whether he shall play with this toy or that, study law or medicine, eat fish or fowl, wear a red or a white hat—which does he account more favorably? Which will give him the greatest satisfaction, cause him the least discomfort, taking into consideration all the influences that bear upon the matter? Even when he chooses an "I don't care" course—or self-abnegation—he is constantly called upon to make decisions in support of this course.

Whether man's decisions are right or wrong, whether what he thinks most desirable is indeed most harmful, or in the end yields him an inadequate return for the amount of exertion invested, is beyond the present point. Ignorance undoubtedly affects his judgment, and limitations put upon him by circumstances and heredity also play their part. The fact remains that his life consists of a sequence of choices, that value is his constant guide in the search for a better and fuller existence.

Shall we conclude that his membership in Society is not a matter of choice, but a miraculous occurrence? Was it predestination or a mere animal impulse which impelled the second frontiersman to become a neighbor of the first? Or was it an act of judgment based on his sense of value? From the viewpoint of political science, and having in mind the ethical validity of political coercion, the question is: does Society result from the will of man or the will of God?

When we consider the profits of cooperative association—of which man is a fair judge—the calling in of divine intent is gratuitous, and perhaps mischievously so. Man is the miracle, but his institutions are wholly rational. Society began when man hit upon the benefits of specialization and trade. This is not to say that he became a Society man contractually, just as one might join a club; it is rather his will to live that impels him to partake of the benefits of the market place. It is the human sense of value that welds a herd of individuals into a cooperating group.

* If this were a book on economics, it would be necessary here to enter into a discussion of money. But that would be outside the scope of this inquiry. Nor is the subject of value, to which this chapter is devoted, fully exploited, as a student of economics might expect, but is treated only as an explanatory note on social and political institutions.

* The theory that the value of a thing is determined by the labor spent in producing it falls flat when we reflect on the things of value that cannot be produced—that have no "cost of production"—such as land sites, patents, monopoly privileges, or heirlooms.

* An illustrative experience is in point. A salesman was offering an expensive suit of wool underwear to a farmer in the wool-growing section of South Dakota. It was in the depression fall of 1934, when labor brought meager returns. The prospective purchaser was as taciturn as the salesman was voluble. The latter thought to bring the business to a close by asking, "What do you say, John?" John replied: ' I've been thinking how many pounds of wool I have to give up to get a suit of this underwear." He was weighing his desire for comfort against its cost in terms of his labor. Maybe he was weighing his desire for comfort against his family's desire for food. His worth as a human being was involved.

CHAPTER 6

The Humanity of Trade

WHEREVER TWO BOYS swap tops for marbles, that is the market place. The simple barter, in terms of human happiness, is no different from a trade transaction involving banking operations, insurance, ships, railroads, wholesale and retail establishments; for in any case the effect and purpose of trade is to make up a lack of satisfactions. The boy with a pocketful of marbles is handicapped in the enjoyment of life by his lack of tops, while the other is similarly discomfited by his need for marbles; both have a better time of it after the swap. In like manner, the Detroit worker who has helped to pile up a heap of automobiles in the warehouse is none the better off for his efforts until the product has been shipped to Brazil in exchange for his morning cup of coffee. Trade is nothing but the release of what one has in abundance to obtain some other thing one wants. It is as pertinent for the buyer to say "thank you" as for the seller.

The market place is not necessarily a specific site, although every trade must take place somewhere. It is more exactly a system of channeling goods or services from one worker to another, from fabricator to consumer, from where a superfluity exists to where there is a need. It is a method devised by man in his pursuit of happiness to diffuse satisfactions, and operating only by the human instinct of value. Its function is not only to transfer ownership from one person to another, but also to direct the current of human exertion; for the price indicator on the chart of the market place registers the desires of people, and the intensity of these desires, so that other people (looking to their own profit) may know how best to employ themselves.

Living without trade may be possible, but it would hardly be living; at best it would be mere existence. Until the market place appears, men are reduced to getting by with what they can find in nature in the way of food and raiment; nothing more. But the will to live is not merely a craving for existence; it is rather an urge to reach out in all directions for a fuller enjoyment of life, and it is by trade that this inner drive achieves some measure of fulfillment. The greater the volume and fluidity of market-place transactions the higher the wage level of Society; and, insofar as things and services make for happiness, the higher the wage level the greater the fund of happiness.

The importance of the market place to the enjoyment of life is illustrated by a custom recorded by Franz Oppenheimer in *The State*. In ancient times, on days designated as holy, the market place and its approaches were held inviolable even by professional robbers; in fact, stepping out of character, these robbers acted as policemen for the trade routes, seeing to it that merchants and caravans were not molested. Why? Because they had accumulated a superfluity of loot of one kind, more than they could consume, and the easiest way of transmuting it into other satisfactions was through trade. Too much of anything is too much.

The market place serves not only to diffuse the abundances that human specialization makes possible, but it is also a distributor of the munificences of nature. For, in her inscrutable way, nature has spread the raw materials by which humans live over the face of the globe; unless some way were devised for distributing these raw materials, they would serve no human purpose. Thus, through the conduit of trade the fish of the sea reach the miner's table and fuel from the inland mine or well reaches the boiler of the fishing boat; tropical fruits are made available to northerners, whose iron mines, translated into tools, make production easier in the tropics. It is by trade that the far-flung warehouses of nature are made accessible to all the peoples of the world and life on this planet becomes that much more enjoyable.

We think of trade as the barter of tangible things simply because that is obvious. But a correlative of the exchange of things is the exchange of ideas, of the knowledge and cultural accumulations of the parties to the transaction. In fact, embodied in the goods is the intelligence of the producers; the excellent woolens imported from England carry evidence of thought that has been given to the art of weaving, and Japanese silks arouse curiosity as to the ideas that went into their fabrication. We acquire knowledge of people through the goods we get from them. Aside from that correlative of trade, there is the fact that trading involves human contacts; and when humans meet, either physically or by means of communication, ideas are exchanged. "Visiting" is the oil that lubricates every market-place operation.

It was only after Cuba and the Philippines were drawn into our trading orbit that interest in the Spanish language and customs was enlivened, and the interest increased in proportion to the volume of our trade with South America. As a consequence, Americans of the present generation are as familiar with Spanish dancing and music as their forefathers, under the influence of commercial contacts with Europe, were at home with the French minuet and the Viennese waltz. When ships started coming from Japan, they brought with them stories of an interesting people, stories that enriched our literature, broadened our art concepts, and added to our operatic repertoire.

It is not only that trading in itself necessitates some understanding of the customs of the people one trades with, but that the cargoes have a way of arousing curiosity as to their source, and ships laden with goods are followed with others carrying explorers of ideas; the open port is a magnet for the curious. So, the tendency of trade is to break down the narrowness of provincialism, to liquidate the mistrust of ignorance. Society, then, in its most comprehensive sense, includes all who for the improvement of their several circumstances engage in trade with one another; its ideational character tends toward a blend of the heterogeneous cultures of the traders. The market place unifies Society.

The concentration of population determines the character of Society only because contiguity facilitates exchange. But contiguity is a relative matter, depending on the means for making contacts; the neutralization of time and space by mechanical means makes the whole world contiguous. The isolationism that breeds an ingrown culture and a mistrust of outside cultures melts away as faster ships, faster trains, and faster planes bring goods and ideas from the great beyond. The perimeter of Society is not fixed by political frontiers but by the radius of its commercial contacts. All people who trade with one another are by that very act brought into community.

The point is emphasized by the strategy of war. The first objective of a general staff is to destroy the market-place mechanisms of the enemy; the destruction of his army is only incidental to that purpose. The army could well enough be left intact if his internal means of communication were destroyed, his ports of entry immobilized, so that specialized production, which depends on trade, could no longer be carried on; the people, reduced to primitive existence, thus lose the will to war and sue for peace. That is the general pattern of all wars. The more highly integrated the economy the stronger will be the nation in war, simply because of its ability to produce an abundance of both military implements and economic goods; on the other hand, if its ability to produce is destroyed, if the flow of goods is interrupted, the more susceptible to defeat it is, because its people, unaccustomed as they are to primitive conditions, are the more easily discouraged. There is no point to the argument as to whether "guns" or "butter" is more important in the prosecution of war.

It follows that any interference with the operation of the market place, however done, is analogous to an act of war. A tariff is such an act.

When we are "protected" against Argentine beef, the effect (as intended) is to make beef harder to get, and that is exactly what an invading army would do. Since the duty does not diminish our desire for beef, we are compelled by the diminished supply to put out more labor to satisfy that desire; our range of possibilities is foreshortened, for we are faced with the choice of getting along with less beef or abstaining from the enjoyment of some other "good." The absence of a plenitude of meat from the market place lowers the purchasing power of our labor. We are poorer, even as is a nation whose ports have been blockaded.

Moreover, since every buyer is a seller, and vice versa, the prohibition against their beef makes it difficult for Argentineans to buy our automobiles, and this expression of our skills is constricted. The effect of a tariff is to drive a potential buyer out of the market place. The argument that "protection' provides jobs is patently fallacious. It is the consumer who gives the worker a job, and the consumer who is prevented from consuming might as well be dead, as far as providing productive employment is concerned.

Incidentally, is it jobs we want, or is it beef? Our instinct is to get the most out of life with the least expenditure of labor. We labor only because we want; the opportunity to produce is not a boon, it is a necessity. Neither the domestic nor the foreign producer "dumps" anything into our laps. There is a price on everything we want and the price is always the weariness of toil. Whatever causes us to put out more toil to acquire a given amount or kind of satisfactions is undesirable, for it conflicts with our natural urge for a more abundant life. Such is a tariff, an embargo, an import quota or the modern device of raising the price of foreign goods by arbitrarily lowering the value of our money. Any restriction of trade, internal or external, does violence to a man's primordial drive to improve his circumstances.

Just as trade brings people together, tending to minimize cultural differences, and makes for mutual understanding, so do impediments to trade have the opposite effect. If the customer is always "right," it is easy to assume that there is something wrong with the nonbuyer. The faults of those who refuse to do business with us are accentuated not only by our loss but also by the sting of personal affront. Should the boy with the tops refuse to trade with the boy who has marbles, they can no longer play together; and this desocialization can easily stir up an argument over the relative demerits of their dogs or parents. Just so, for all our protestations of good neighborliness, the Argentinean has his doubts about our intentions when we bolt our commercial doors against him; compelled to look elsewhere for more substantial friendship, he is inclined to think less of our national character and culture.

The by-product of trade isolationism is the feeling that the "outsider" is a "different kind" of person, and therefore inferior, with whom social contact is at least undesirable if not dangerous. To what extent this segregation of people by trade restrictions is the cause of war is a moot question, but there can be no doubt that such restrictions are irritants that can give other causes for war more plausibility; it makes no sense to attack a good customer, one who buys as much of our products as he can use and pays his bills regularly. Perhaps the removal of trade restrictions throughout the world would do more for the cause of universal peace than can any political union of peoples separated by trade barriers; indeed, can there be a viable political union while these barriers exist? And, if freedom of trade were the universal practice, would a political union be necessary?

Let us test the claims of "protectionists" with an experiment in logic. If a people prosper by the amount of foreign goods they are *not* permitted to have, then a complete embargo, rather than a restriction, would do them the most good. Continuing that line of reasoning, would it not be better all around if each community were hermetically sealed off from its neighbor, like Philadelphia from New York? Better still, would not every household have more on its table if it were compelled to live on its own production? Silly as this *reductio ad absurdum* is, it is no sillier than the "protectionist" argument that a nation is enriched by the amount of foreign goods it keeps out of its market, or the "balance of trade" argument that a nation prospers by the excess of its exports over imports.

Yet, if we detach ourselves mentally from entrenched myths, we see that acts of internal isolationism such as described in our syllogism are not infrequent. A notorious instance of this is the French *octroi*, a tax levied on products entering one district from another. Under cover of "quarantine" regulations, Florida and California have mutually excluded citrus fruits grown in the other state. Labor unions are violent advocates of opulence-through-scarcity, as when they restrict, by direct violence or by laws they have had enacted, the importation of materials made outside their jurisdiction. A tax on trucks entering one state from another is of a piece with this line of reasoning. Thus, the "protectionist" theory of fence building is internalized, and in the light of these facts our *reductio ad absurdum* is not so farfetched. The market place, of course, scoffs at such scarcity-making measures, for it yields no more than it receives; if its offerings are made scarce by trade restrictions, that which remains becomes harder to get, calls for an expenditure of more labor to acquire. The wage level of Society is lowered.

The myth of "protectionism" rests on the notion that the be-all and end-all of human life is laboring, not consumption—and certainly not leisure. If that were so, then the slaves who built pyramids were most ideally situated; they worked much and received little. Likewise, the Russians chained to "five-year plans" have achieved heaven on earth, and so did the workers who, during the depression, were put to moving dirt from one side of the road to the other. Extending this notion that exertion for the sake of exertion is the way to prosperity, then a people would be most prosperous if they all labored on projects with no reference to their individual sense of value. What is euphemistically called "war production ' is a case in point; there is in fact no such thing, since the purpose of production is consumption; and it is not on record that any worker built a battleship because he wanted it and proved his craving by willingly giving up anything in exchange for it. Keeping in mind the exaltation of laboring, would not a people be most uplifted if they all were set to building battleships, nothing else, in return for the necessaries that would enable them to keep on building battleships? They certainly would not be unemployed.

Yet, if we base our thinking on the natural urge of the individual to better his circumstances and widen his horizon, operating always under the natural law of parsimony (the most gain for the least effort), we are compelled to the conclusion that effort which does not add to the abundance of the market place is useless effort. Society thrives on trade simply because trade makes specialization possible, specialization increases output, and increased output reduces the cost in toil for the satisfactions men live by. That being so, the market place is a most humane institution.

CHAPTER 7

Plenty by Competition

THE TECHNIQUES of the market place evolve from mans unceasing drive toward a richer and fuller life. One technique that plays a most important part in this general purpose is competition, or the vying among the specialists for the favor of the community. Although the competitors are motivated by self-interest, each one seeking the custom of his fellow men, the effect of the rivalry is to bring an abundance into the market place, to the greater benefit of Society. To win favor for his offerings, as against the offerings of others in the same line, each competitor tries to improve his capacity for production, as to quantity or quality; each seeks to better his competence.

But, what is competence, and how is it determined by those whose trade is sought? Getting down to the bedrock of definitions, competence is a grade of performance, and as the word is generally used it designates a high grade. Its opposite is incompetence, a low grade, and in between there must be a number of gradations. A performance is good or bad, competent or incompetent, only in comparison with other performances.

If Smith is the only cobbler in town, and we are unacquainted with the workmanship of cobblers in other towns, how can we judge his skill? The best we can do under the circumstances is to compare his performance with what we could do for ourselves as amateur cobblers; before he came, that was the best service we had. Let us concede that our monopoly cobbler is a decent fellow and that he does the best he can for our footwear. But he is under no compulsion to do better, and his best may be determined by his conscience or the state of his health. Like the rest of us, he dislikes the irksomeness and weariness of toil and tries to get by with the minimum of effort. Since we cannot take our trade elsewhere, and Smith is aware of this, his natural inclination is to take a let-well-enough-alone attitude toward his workmanship, and in fixing his prices he follows the rule of "all the traffic will bear." The only restraint on his monopoly impulse is the possibility of driving his customers to self-help cobbling and losing their trade.

Only when Brown opens a rival shop in town is Smith compelled to look to and prove his competence. To attract trade the newcomer either undercuts the erstwhile monopolist or improves on the quality of his work;

the latter retaliates by offering to sole shoes "while you wait"; Brown invents, or buys from an inventor, a machine enabling him to cut his labor costs, turn out more jobs in a given time, and therefore to charge less than Brown; and so it goes. Each improves his performance in some way, not out of compassion for his customers but out of regard for his own well-being. Nevertheless, it is the community that profits by the rising standard and shows its appreciation by patronizing the specialist who, all things considered, serves their interests best. They applaud the performance, not the performer.

The practical measurement of competence is the profit-and-loss statement of the competitor, for in it are recorded the favorable or unfavorable votes of the Society he serves. Thus, the income of the auto mechanic reflects the repairs he has effected, the profits of the manufacturer prove his ability to produce what is wanted, the salary of the managerial genius comes off the production line. Each has been rewarded by Society for his performance, as compared with the performances of his competitors, and his gain is proof enough that Society has gained. It follows then that a Society of affluent competitors is one in which the wage level, or the general fund of satisfactions, is high.

The coming of Brown may be a benefit to the community, but to Smith it is a discomfit. Heretofore, his craftsmanship and the price he charged for his service were fixed by his own convenience, but now he is compelled to meet standards set by another. The monopoly impulse in him, which he shares with all human beings, is disturbed. Therefore, Smith is inclined to prevent Brown from offering his competitive service to his trade and under primitive conditions might resort to arms. Since a growing Society frowns upon such crude methods, he turns to a more sophisticated use of force, that of convincing his neighbors that scarcity in some way improves their lot; that "home industry" should be encouraged; that Brown is an inferior human being and therefore a detriment to the community; that lower prices endanger the "general economy." Perhaps his argument is convincing because each of his neighbors entertains the hope of a monopoly position of his own, of getting something for nothing; at any rate, he succeeds in using collective force to achieve his private purpose. And thus come scarcity-producing laws, such as protective tariffs, exclusion acts, prohibitions on labor-saving devices, restraints on trade, or a tax on enterprise. Either Brown is prevented from offering his services to the community, or his goods are kept out of the market place, or a tax is levied on his improved machinery—or maybe a labor union prevents him from using it. It is by force that Smith retains his comfortable monopoly position; it is by force that competition is prevented from enriching the market place.

It is an odd circumstance that such scarcity-producing measures are not self-enforcing, simply because the monopoly impulse is counterbalanced by the stronger urge of the human for abundance, and the conflict results in lawbreaking by the very law passers. Thus comes the practice of smuggling, of tax evasion, of bootlegging, as well as the resort to substitutes for the product made scarce by monopoly. It is not surprising that Smith's neighbors, who helped him avoid competition, avail themselves by devious methods of Brown's services.

When a monopoly position is achieved, when competition is eliminated or restrained, competence has a new meaning. It no longer designates a standard of performance fixed in the market place. The monopolist, the one who controls the supply of a desirable commodity or service, regulates his performance by a neat formula: the highest price which will yield him the highest net profit. If he increases the output beyond a predetermined point, he must lower the price so as to induce greater consumption, and nothing is gained. If he increases the price, consumption will fall and so will his net profit. Competence in a monopoly therefore consists in finding (by the trial-and-error method) the exact profit-yielding ratio between price and performance. The profit-and-loss statement of a monopoly business reflects only in part the service it has rendered Society; it also includes an exaction price made possible by the scarcity it is able to cause.*

The key to monopoly is scarcity. Some scarcities are natural, such as mineral deposits and land sites; there is no way for humans to duplicate them. The ownership or control of these limited opportunities to produce enables the monopolist to exact a rent price for the use of them. The rent price is fixed by their relative scarcity—or by the yield of any given site over that of any other site available to use. In point of fact, the rent price is fixed by competition among users or producers for exclusive possession of these locations.

Other scarcities are made by law, and the mechanism by which these scarcities are effected is always a coercive restriction on competition. Although the restrictive measures are sometimes concocted by individuals or groups in search of a monopoly price, these are of little effect unless and until they are implemented with the strong arm of the law, as when it imposes trade regulations, tries to fix prices, subsidizes inefficient producers at the expense of efficient ones, enables labor organizations to put limits on enterprise, or grants special privileges to favored individuals. This brings us to a consideration of the part played by the political organization of Society in its economy, which we must leave to a later chapter. For the present, we leave the matter with this observation: there cannot be an effective blocking of man's urge for abundance through competition without the aid of the law. That is, every scarcity-making device rests on political coercion.

Indeed, those who decry competition on pseudohumanitarian grounds look to the law to restrain competition, even as they call upon the law to prevent the monopoly exactions made possible by such restraint. Their argument is that those who are possessed of less ability are handicapped in the competitive struggle and will be hurt unless the more competent are shackled. (Sometimes they urge the discouragement of initiative by proposing that the profits which bring out initiative be taxed away, sometimes they contemplate the impossible task of rooting out the profit motive altogether.) But how can any member of Society be hurt by an abundance in the market place? If Brown, because of his greater skill or industry, takes shoe business away from Smith, his success is proof that he has rendered a greater service to the members of the community; they are the better off because of his efficiency. He has produced better shoes, or a greater variety of styles and sizes, or through improved methods has lowered his costs and reduced prices. But his efficiency is meaningless unless they buy his shoes; buying his shoes means that they have produced something he wants. That is to say, any increase in the production of one desirable thing calls for the production of other desirable things. In the case of Brown, his burgeoning shoe business necessitates the production of more shoe findings, shoe boxes, and other incidentals, to say nothing of stimulating such services as transportation, book-keeping, selling; furthermore, he must employ more people in his operation. In this profusion of activity, Smith is sure to find a remunerative occupation of some kind, and though his pride may suffer because he had not been able to keep up with the standard set by Brown, his well-being may have been improved. The old adage has it that "competition is good for business," and when business is "good" all Society prospers.

The anticompetition advocates like to stress the point that large aggregations of capital put the "little fellow" at a disadvantage; because of the means at his disposal the "big fellow" is able to buy raw materials in large quantities and therefore at a lower price, to put in the most advanced machinery, to invest in expensive selling campaigns. Quite true. Putting aside the fact that all this merely means greater production for the benefit of Society, the record shows that bigness in itself imposes restrictions on production; the ponderous plant lacks the flexibility necessary to meet the vagaries of human desire. Brown, the large shoe manufacturer, cannot cater to the foot that does not conform to some norm or to the whims of the fastidious wearer. His plant is geared to mass production. It is Smith, who either did not choose to become a manufacturer or was not adapted for the role, who must serve this clientele, which always grows in proportion to the increase of wealth in the community; the number of small plants or "specialty shops" keeps pace with the number and size of large industrial units. In fact, the large plant admits its limitations when it turns over to its smaller competitor the jobs it cannot do as efficiently.

There is nothing wrong with competition that competition cannot cure. The faults of competition are in the impediments that are put in its way by force—the restraints, taxes, and regulations that handicap some competitors and give others a monopoly or quasi-monopoly position. Competition serves Society best when it is free. In the field of cultural satisfactions no one would propose that competition be shackled, that the better singer be compelled to perform under poorer acoustic conditions than those afforded the second-rater, or that the discrepancies in artistic ability be equalized by law. There is common agreement that in those occupations the impartial verdict of the market place is final, even if it decides that the inferior ballplayer would better serve Society, and himself, by driving a truck. Since the expectation of material rewards (the profit motive) plays a big part in stimulating desirable competition among these cultural specialists, it should follow that competition among those engaged in the production of material things is equally desirable. The artist also seeks to satisfy his desires with the minimum of effort.

On the score of humanitarianism, free competition commends itself on the ground that those who are necessarily outside the field of production, or partly so, are in better case in an economy of plenty than in an economy of scarcity. The physically handicapped, the children, and the aged must in any event be taken care of, and their lot is better in a household where the pantry is full.

To repeat, this does not pretend to be a book on economics. It is rather an attempt to show that economics plays a big, if not major, part in the formation and development of social integrations and institutions, and toward that end it was necessary to outline, broadly, the economic principles which bear upon the thesis.

Any inquiry into the nature of or reason for Society (and its attendant political institutions) must begin with an examination of its integer, the individual. Any other approach would be like starting in mid-air. But the individual proves to be a rather complicated phenomenon, with variable and elusive characteristics, casting a variegated light on his social habits. We must put these aside and seek in the evidence of his behavior, throughout history and wherever we find him, a constant pattern. This, and there can be no question about it, is his life-long preoccupation with the making of a living. His will to live compels him to be the "economic man." Even the nonmaterial facets of his makeup—meta-physical, cultural, and spiritual—are in one manner or another tied in with the way he goes about making his living. The constancy of his concern with economics indicates that it must be the foundation on which he builds his social environment; all else is superstructure.

Society, then, is basically an economic phenomenon. It is an aggregation of individuals who, by means of the techniques emerging from cooperation, better their circum-stances. It is a means of raising the general wage level; if it did not effect that result it would tend to disintegrate. The social integrations we call primitive are those in which the economic techniques have not been developed, for one reason or another, while the advanced Society is one that exploits them as fully as the cooperators know how. A perfect Society, or one as perfect as human knowledge can make it, would be one where these techniques, collectively called the market place, operated without friction; this, the world has not yet seen, for reasons that will be explored in the following chapters.

* The competitor, like the monopolist, seeks the highest price which will yield him the highest net profit. But, because he is unable to control supply, and thus induce a scarcity, his highest price is what competition will allow him to charge, which is always lower than what he would like. In a competitive business, the net profit breaks down to interest on investment, replacement of capital, and the wages of superintendence. Only in a monopoly business is there a "little extra.

CHAPTER 8

Government and Property

AS EVERYONE KNOWS, an analogy is neither evidence nor proof. And yet, since Aristotle it has been common practice among political scientists to call upon an analogy to support a theory of the origin of Government; namely, that Government grew out of the organization of the family. There is, of course, no historical evidence of a cause-and-effect relationship between the two institutions; all that we have is an un-proven hypothesis, resting on an assumed similarity between parental authority and Government authority. The hypothesis disproves itself, however, when the biological factor in parental authority is taken into consideration. The child looks to the parent for guidance simply because of the inadequacies and insecurity of childhood, and seeks or accepts authority as a matter of necessity. Government has no such claim on its citizenry, nor is loyalty to it in any way analogous to filial devotion. Even the father-son relationship alters in character as the offspring reaches maturity and attains self-sufficiency, a relationship in which authority diminishes and disappears; the citizen's allegiance to Government is unrelated to his age or to his ability to take care of himself. Neat as the analogy is, it does not bear up under analysis and one must look elsewhere for some explanation of the phenomenon of Government.

We get some hint as to the reason for Government when we look to the emergence of this institution from embryonic Society, the one that sprang up on our western frontier. In the beginning, when our pioneers settled down to the business of making a living in the wilderness, the minuscule Society got along without any organized authority. The best there was, was individual authority, as represented by the gun which each pioneer kept at hand. To be sure, the primary function of this instrument was that of capital, a tool to facilitate the securing of food for the table or pelts for the wardrobe. Its use, however, was not confined to this productive purpose; when occasion arose, the pioneer resorted to it to protect life and property, and when so used the purpose was to oppose his will to that of the depredator. It was his authority against that of another.

Government is authority, and authority, in this sense, is the imposition of one's will on that of another, so as to induce behavior deemed desirable or to prevent behavior deemed undesirable. Regardless of the form of Government, whether the authority is exercised by a chief or a monarch or an elected official, whether the purpose is to satisfy his whim or to enforce a law, whether or not it has the sanction of public opinion, the action itself is the opposition of volition against volition. And even though the authority is accepted and readily complied with, it is the use or threat of force that gives authority its substance. Therefore, when the frontiersman made use of his gun to thwart the purposes of a depredator he was in effect acting as Government; he was exercising such force as he had at his disposal to compel compliance with his will.

He was protecting life and property. The value the individual puts on life is instinctive and primordial, and his concern with its preservation needs no other explanation. But why his interest in property, with something outside of him? Why does he endanger his life or undergo hardship in order to keep and enjoy property? That calls for a definition of property and an understanding of the individual's relationship to it, which we will take up later. For the present, we need only observe that organized Government does not make its appearance until property becomes a factor in social integrations, and its authority is called upon more and more as property becomes more important in the pursuit of happiness; hence the concept of Government and the concept of property are interrelated. Would there be any need for Government if the individual had no sense of property, no concern with ownership?

The primary concern of the pioneer is with production; the need for disengaging himself from production to pursue some protective enterprise is a nuisance; there is no profit in it. The time and effort put into policing the competence piled up in his barn and pantry could be better employed, and the thought occurs to him that it would be more profitable for him to turn over his gun, his instrument of authority, to a specialist in its use. His neighbors are of like mind. Sad experience has taught them that the abundances they have accumulated are a magnet for people who seek to satisfy their desires with no investment of toil, and the concern of each with his property becomes a common concern. Thus comes the posse and the vigilante committee, the instrument of collective security. The essential feature of this instrument is the use of force to prevent behavior inimical to their business of making a living. That is Government. It is a social service established by the members of the community to do that which each would do for himself if he could, and which he is compelled to do for himself before there are a sufficient number of producers in the community to hire a specialist.

Volunteer Government does for a while. But the interruptive call to duty becomes more strident as the community grows in size and in wealth, and in due time voluntarism is replaced with a professional sheriff, whose keep is less costly than the stoppage of production. By contract, he is relieved from contributing anything to the market place, from which he draws his sustenance, in return for which he agrees to devote his time and talents to maintaining the orderly conditions necessary for the smooth operation of the market place. He renders a special service to the community, differing from all the others in that its sole purpose is the exercise of authority; as sheriff he is not equipped for any productive occupation, nor has he any competence for one. Government is a protector, not a producer.*

For illustrative purposes, we have inferred that the horse thief or the cattle rustler is an outsider, not a member of the community. But what is a thief—psychologically, not legally? He is a man who turns to predation rather than production to satisfy his desires, convinced that his way calls for a minimum of exertion. Because he is uninhibited by a moral sense or the fear of punishment, he is described as a psychopath. Whether he is or not, the fact is that he shares with all his fellow men the inclination to get "something for nothing," his deficiency being but an exaggeration of the common impulse. The coveting of somebody else's property is not confined to the practicing thief but is a characteristic of the human being, and therefore in every community quarrels arise over the question of ownership, all the more so as the intricacies of trade develop. In the interest of that tranquillity without which production becomes difficult, to the discouragement of accumulations, the community sets up an impartial third party to adjudicate these and all other disputes. The tribunal is Government. Thus, the institution that grew out of the need for a protector of property takes on the related duty of judge.

The policeman-judge institution makes its appearance soon after every Society is born, and along with it there emerges from the experience of the group a set of rules of behavior for the guidance of its members, all to the end that the pursuit of happiness shall be facilitated; the occupation of this institution is to see that these rules are observed. This singularity of Government sets it off from all the specialized services that make up Society. To repeat, Society consists of a number of producers, each contributing to the general fund of wealth, and each depending for acceptance of his goods or services on the free vote of the market place; he has no power of compulsion. Government too is a specialized service, differing from all the others in that it contributes nothing tangible to the market place and is endowed with the monopoly of coercion. That is the peculiar characteristic of Government wherever we find it; by common consent it enjoys a monopoly of coercion so that it can prevent the indiscriminate exercise of coercion by the members of the community. It cannot be subjected to the competitive conditions that promote productive enterprise, because competitive coercion is competitive violence, the very condition that Government is intended to remove. Government must be monopolistic.

When Society is primitive—that is, specialization is not developed and therefore production is limited—the coercive power of Government is restricted to public opinion. A prime example is that of the American Indian tribe, in which the chief was indeed the policeman-judge, vested with authority to interpret the traditional code, but depending on social sanctions for the execution of his dicta. He had no other enforcement agency. A more notable example is that of the Israelite constitution before the advent of kings. The tribes were held together by a voluntary covenant, and behavior was regulated by a code called *mishpat*, or justice; it was a set of rules that came out of the crucible of experience. Disputes among the tribesmen were referred to judges, men who attained the post by their reputation for wisdom and integrity. While they seem to have had no political authority, no power of coercion, they constituted effective Government because their judgment was automatically enforced by the tribesmen themselves. Even after the kingship was established, against the advice of Samuel, their chief judge, it was not granted the right of legislation, since God was the only recognized lawgiver.

"Thus," observes Lord Acton, "the example of the Hebrew nation laid down the parallel lines along which all freedom has been won—the doctrine of national tradition and the doctrine of a higher law; the principle that a constitution grows from the root, by a process of development, and not by essential change; and the principle that all political authorities must be tested and reformed according to a code which was not made by man."

Government does not have much to do in a simple economy; that is because there is not enough produced to arouse cupidity. Internal squabbles are relatively few and unimportant, and the poverty of the tribe is reasonable assurance that no one will attack it. Trouble begins when accumulations appear. It is then that Government is called upon to assume a major role in Society, a role that would not be difficult to perform if reason were to provide it with a clear-cut, moral definition of property. For that we must look to the behavior of the individual: why does he put such weight on ownership, and what does his claim rest upon? More specifically, on what grounds does he expect Government to guarantee his claim to property?

And the individual replies with an axiom: he has a right to live. Whether he has or not is neither provable nor disputable: all reasoning on the subject leads to the dead-end of all causality, "the nature of things." By this hypothesis, the individual has a right to life simply because he craves it. Who can dispute that point without throwing doubt on his own right to existence?

The right to life, or the right to oneself, must mean the exclusive title to all the faculties which are identifiable with that thing called "me": body, mind, appetites, aspirations, all the factors of personality. This peculiar bundle of flesh and soul is "mine," first, because it came into existence when "I" was born, an act of God, and will pass out of existence when "I" die; secondly, there is no way of transferring title to that personality to anyone who is not "me." That is the important point, that neither science nor politics is capable of devising a way of transforming "I" into "he" or "we." Oneself is oneself throughout life.

Now, title to life is not merely metaphysical; its reality is the enjoyment of those things which, according to the dictates of nature, make life possible. Without them, "me" disappears. The raw material for those things are all about "me," put there by the same intelligence that put "me" on this earth. But it so happens that this profusion of life-giving materials serves "me" inadequately until it is transformed into consumable shape. "Me" must go to work on those things so as to make them contributory to life; and though "me" finds labor wearisome and undesirable, so strong is the will to life that this aversion is overcome. Thus, some part of "me" is invested in what "I" wanted to enjoy; it would not have existed and could not be enjoyed unless that investment of labor were made. It is by virtue of this investment of "me" that the desirable thing becomes "mine." It is "mine" because "I" made it.

Title to things, or the right of property, enjoys moral validity, therefore, only when it rests on labor.* Any other theory of property rights must begin by rejecting the right of the individual to himself and must assume that the successful use of force to separate the producer from his product is title enough. Putting aside moral considerations, title resting on the use of force is transitory, vague, and uncertain, because it must change with every change in the incidence of force. Thus, the slave owner enjoys the chattel's property only so long as he can exert force on the slave; when the slave overthrows his master, the title to property reverts to the former slave. The thief becomes an honest man and the honest man a thief according to which is stronger. Whenever we invoke a rule of property that does not recognize the relationship between the producer and his product, we are involved in contradictions; we are on transitory grounds and outside the field of principle.

When we recognize the employment of force in acquiring property—that is, when our sense of reality has not been dulled by adjustment to its employment—we are quick to put upon it the stamp of inequity; we call it exploitation, confiscation, appropriation, thievery. It is a *malum in se*, an inherently evil act. In that way we assert the conviction that depriving the producer of the fruits of his efforts is an infringement of his right to life. It is an immoral act. And it is an immoral act even if it is sanctioned by law or is committed by a number of people acting in concert, for there is no multiplier large enough to make a wrong a right. When we consider the consequences of the substitution of a forceful (or legal) for a moral right to property, as we will, we shall see that the violation of principle cannot be done with impunity. But, on principle alone, regardless of consequences, any method, legal or illegal, by which title to property is shifted from producer to nonproducer, is essentially akin to the burglarizing of a house. Under letters of marque issued by the monarch, piracy became privateering, but in either case it was stealing; and when I am compelled against my will to support a school or a bureaucracy, under any pretext, I am being deprived of my property.

Judgment on the soundness or desirability of an act or procedure must take into account its consequences; and a theory must prove itself in practice. When we put this theory—that the right of property rests on labor—to the test of experience, we find that it is supported by what might be called a natural law; that is, an invariable cause-and-effect relationship that operates automatically, undeterred by human will and enabling us to make predictions. The law may be stated thus: the worker's possession and enjoyment, including disposition, of his past production determine the amount of his future production; or, the level of consumption (wages) determines the level of production.

It is admitted that what has already been produced may be alienated from the producer, and nature interposes no automatic restraints. That is to say, so long as it is possible by legal or illegal methods to shift possession physically, there is no imperative relationship between production and consumption; one can consume what another has produced. But this fact applies to past production only and does not take into account the continuing process of production. It should be kept in mind that the object of production is the satisfaction of desires and that desires do not cease until life ends. Man exerts labor in order that he may consume the output, and if he is frustrated in his purpose, what will be the effect on his future efforts? There can be no question as to the answer. The only point at issue is whether the consequent curtailment of effort is an act of will or is as automatic as, say, the rise and fall of tides. If it is an act of will, then the use of force will keep production going in spite of the thievery; but if it is "in the nature of things" that production must drop in the amount of defalcation practiced, then all the king's men and horses will not keep the productive machinery going.

In a primitive economy there is no difficulty in tracing the relationship between production and consumption. For here the worker culls directly from nature and the identity of his exertion with his property is clearly evident. He eats the animal he slaughters, the grain he grows; he wears the hides and the pelts he gathers; he keeps warm in a house he built with the wood he brings in from the forest. Every effort he puts forth, either in obtaining his necessaries or in piling up capital for the future, redounds to his benefit. He makes his own wages. If nature responds abundantly to his efforts—since he is never lacking in desires—he keeps on investing more and more of himself in property.

However, if the pioneer's property is ravaged by pests or destroyed by droughts, floods, and earthquakes, he will migrate elsewhere, and in that case his shop closes down, production ceases; or he will put forth effort to overcome the hazards, and in that case production is lessened by the amount of effort put into the struggle. If robbers threaten his possessions he must likewise make a nonprofitable expenditure of effort in protection at the expense of output. Likewise, that part of his wages which he must give up for permission to live, say to tax collectors or anyone else having an enforceable claim on his output, is really not his; since he does not have it he cannot invest it in satisfactions. His will has nothing to do with the matter. The conditions which bring about a lessening of property cause a comparable diminution of production; the effort expended in baling out the boat does not speed it on its appointed course.

Operation of the law of property is more clearly evident when we look into indirect or money wages. Here a time lag between production and consumption dissolves all appearance of intent. Let us follow through a specific instance. A clothing worker acquires title to a coat by virtue of the labor he has put into it; even municipal law acknowledges the morality of his title by way of a mechanic's lien. But his economic interest is not in the coat *per se*. He made it not for the purpose of wearing it but with the idea of transferring his title in it to somebody else in exchange for satisfactions he craves. He sells his interest in the coat to the entrepreneur, another worker, by the terms of a wage contract. The entrepreneur likewise has no need for the coat, and the title he acquired to it is also a means to an end. Eventually, the coat reaches its ultimate destination, the desiring consumer. If this one owns goods or tokens of value equivalent to the worth put on the coat in the market place, an exchange takes place and title is transferred to him. No sooner has the new owner put on the coat than it starts to disintegrate, for that is the fate of all labor products. But the coat-desire, the craving for warmth or adornment, does not disintegrate; it is coexistent with life. So, then, the consumption or use of the coat is in itself a signal to the coat factory, to all the specialists in that line, to get busy on a replacement, because a desirer will have property to exchange for it. It is property, the ownership of the fruits of one's labor, that keeps the productive machinery going, automatically and without human intent, unless we identify the will to live with intent. That being so, we can predict that production will always keep pace with the amount of disposable income in the hands of the producers, or that the wealth of Society is in proportion to the property of its members.

Let us consider a negative condition: the would-be coat consumer is without property. The reason is unimportant; either he chose not to produce, or conditions over which he had no control prevented him from producing, or a swindler or a commissar deprived him of his output. He has no property to exchange for the coat he wants. In that case, the coat factory has to shut down; if it continues to make coats we have a condition which economists call "overproduction," but which is really underconsumption. The stoppage is caused not by lack of desire but by a lack of property, and human will, except insofar as it has played a part in depriving the producer of his property, is not responsible for the stoppage. It is automatic: no property, no production.*

This law of property functions even though the exchangeable property is offered by persons who have acquired title to it by theft, chicanery, or gift. As long as they have the unearned property at their disposal, production will continue. Since, however, such persons do not bring to the market place a replacement for the goods they take from it, merely exchanging that which the producer would have exchanged, the productive process is slowed down by the amount of their consumption. Only production begets production; mere consumption, or spending, does not stimulate output. People do not produce for money but for the things that money will buy. If spending alone could keep the market place active, then a Society consisting of profligate thieves would be in better case than one consisting entirely of producers. The idea of opulence through profligacy assumes that consumption is the fuel that keeps a full head of steam in the productive boiler and must be regulated by coercive methods; but consumption will take care of itself, men being what they are, if the productive process is not interrupted by any infringement of the moral right of property.

In the light of this principle, that the level of wages (consumption) is fixed by the level of production, and vice versa, the fact that free labor (labor permitted to enjoy its produce) is more productive than slave labor becomes self-explanatory. An "underprivileged" people is one that is regularly deprived of its property, or one in which the definition of property as anything that under the law may be bought and sold, no matter how obtained, prevails. Contrariwise, a Society is rich, healthy, and vigorous insofar as it refrains from obstructing the individual's search for a fuller life by means of the enjoyment of the fruits of his labor.

It is probably not a *conscious* understanding of the relationship between property and production that gives rise to the need for Government, but rather an *emotional* understanding of it; the indisputable right to life gives one an in-disputable right to the enjoyment of one's output of labor, and some machinery for the safeguarding of this right is deemed necessary. That is the business of Government.

* The argument is sometimes advanced that Government is a producer because its protective function induces a climate conducive to production. This is like saying that the umpire at a baseball game makes runs, hits, and errors, which is manifestly silly. Political power, if it has any competence at all, may regulate human behavior; it is not a factor in production.
* Title to property must include the right to its value, if any. The baker's right to eat the pie he made cannot be questioned. Neither can he be denied the right to accept in exchange for the pie the equivalent of two pies, if anybody should make the offer. The labor theory of property has nothing to do with the labor theory of value.
* Slaves, who are denied the right to own what they produce, will produce something in excess of their consumption wages, either to avoid pain or in the expectation of an increase in wages. If the prospect of punishment or improvement is removed, the slave will produce no more than the sustenance needed for existence.

CHAPTER 9

A Case of Corruption

DIONYSIUS, the storied tyrant of Syracuse, was a consummate financier. His gift stood him in good stead on the day he found himself in bankrupt condition, having borrowed from the citizenry more than he could repay. He might have increased taxes and satisfied his creditors with their own money, but he did not do so because, presumably, his levies had reached the point of diminishing returns; an increase could have discouraged production, or caused a flight of capital, and thus dried up the source of his income. That would not do. And yet, the debts had to be met, since repudiation would have blemished his reputation and impaired the national credit; no one would have lent him a plugged Syracusan dime thereafter.

In this predicament, Dionysius worked out a scheme that has come to the rescue of national profligacy ever since. He called in all the coin of his realm, known as drachmae, restamped them so that each drachma became two, and, after paying off his debts with the revalued money, returned to the owners many more drachmae than they had been obliged to turn in. No doubt, the Syracusans were delighted by the operation; their advances to the tyrant were paid up in full and their nonmonetary assets had suddenly doubled in price. He deserved praise for this financial feat.

In twenty-two centuries men do a lot of thinking, and out of this cerebration come new ways of doing old things. Like Dionysius, latter-day politicians sometimes find themselves without the wherewithal needed to defray the costs of glorious State adventures and, having stretched taxation to the breaking point, resort to borrowing. They convince the citizens not only that their savings will be spent in ways that will redound to their benefit, but that they will be rewarded for their faith with an annual increment; the imposingly printed receipt issued to the lender solemnly pledges the honor of the State to that effect. Now, in one way or another, these receipts become monetized, and Society is deluged with new coin of the realm, even as were the Syracusans when their drachmae were restamped. Everybody is "enriched." This modem financial wizardry is a vast improvement on Dionysius' method in that it conveys the impression of an honest business transaction, not a swindle.

Evidently, Dionysius had not thought of this receipt business, for if he had he would never have found himself in the aforesaid predicament. He would never have been faced with bankruptcy. For, among its other advantages, this modern receipt bears a maturity date, usually falling in the next generation, to the relief of the immediate borrowers; furthermore, through refinancing and funding methods this date acquires the unique capacity of extending itself into eternity, so that the loan need never be repaid. On the other hand, the lender or his offspring can always be sure of receiving interest, since as a taxpayer the holder provides the funds.

We have no doubt that Dionysius' ministers fortified him with a learned dissertation on the virtues of his restamping scheme. His modern counterpart not only has ministers to advise him but also professors of economics to explain to the public how the abundance in their pantries is improved by inflation.

Tax farming went out of style even before the Roman Empire collapsed. Or did it? When we dig into the modern institution of tariffs we come upon by-products that have a resemblance to the ancient institution. To begin with, the despised publicans of Caesarian times performed a function that was not unlike that of the modern customs-house inspectors and collectors, who are, like their forebears, a well-kept and nonproductive element in the population. Then, there is the concomitant of tariffs known as the pyramiding of profits. The importer who pays the tariff must include this amount in his costs, to which is added his normal mark-up in computing his selling price. Each additional handler or processor must do likewise, and if the material brought into the country is in raw form, requiring much handling and processing before it reaches the consumable stage, the various percentages added may come to more than the tariff. The consumer pays all. The gains of these handlers and processors are not unlike the rake-offs of the ancient satraps; they are private profits made possible by law.

We have no authority for it, but knowing that no business can be pursued without moral justification, we can assume that the Roman tax gatherers were convinced of the correctness of their enterprise; did they not bring to the taxpayers the benefits of Roman law and order? Likewise, those who benefit by it espouse the cause of protectionism on the ground that it promotes domestic industry, gives jobs to citizens, protects them from slave-labor competition, and so on. A hold-up cannot look itself in the face.

Since the matter of succession was not constitutionally regularized, the praetorian guard undertook to provide Rome with a steady supply of emperors. (Sometimes the legions set up a claimant of their own, and then the selection was decided by a test of arms.) Admitting that the soldiery considered the course of empire in making their choice, they were nevertheless not uninfluenced by the aspirant's promise to improve their economic welfare. We might call that venal voting, but in what essential does it differ from the promises to veterans that now embellish campaign oratory? Or, notice the emoluments and special advantages the modern politician holds out to conscripts so that they might accept the condition of involuntary servitude in better grace. That the praetorian guard still plays an important part in the selection of our political leaders is evidenced by the fact that for over a generation after the Civil War nearly every candidate for the presidency was a general, and that in every campaign the soldier bonus was an issue; since World War I, no candidate for any office would think of advocating any curtailment of the special advantages which organized veterans deem their due.

The point of the analogy is not that ancient and modern men of arms are alike in their pursuit of something for nothing—in that respect they are no different from the rest of the citizenry—but that in every age political power has lent itself to purposes that are uneconomic and antisocial, that it has never hesitated to purchase support with confiscated property. For the ancients it may be said that they conducted the business in a forthright manner, unadorned with moralisms; the Caesars did not invoke an ideology to cover up the real objective of "bread and circuses," Today, political preferment and the augmentation of political power are accomplished in the same way—with subsidies of all sorts, paid for by taxpayers—but the business is conducted under a panoply of rectitude. Our politicians do not purchase votes, they advocate "social" programs. It comes to the same thing.

History is replete with such illustrative matter, and the temptation is strong to adduce examples showing that only in forms and details have the confiscatory practices of political power undergone change. But, considering the character of authority, what else can it do? Political power is not a factor in production; it cannot contribute a single loaf of bread or pair of shoes to the market place; the things that satisfy human desires result from the application of labor to raw materials, and in that process political power is out of its element. The best it can do to promote production is to maintain a climate of tranquillity. When it undertakes to intervene in the market place it is equipped for nothing else than taking what it finds. The more it takes the less there is for Society to get along on, and the depletion causes an attitude of dependence on the confiscatory power. This attitude is enhanced when selected groups become beneficiaries of the confiscation; they are then beholden to political power for their welfare, and support and adulation of the benefactor is a natural reaction. Political power thrives on confiscation.

To prove the point, it is only necessary to point up the fact that political establishments stick to their negative role when Society produces little, and that they become active and grow in stature only when an accumulation of wealth appears. Among the North American Indian tribes, where production equaled subsistence, the chiefs, who were part-time and volunteer politicians, exercised little authority and that only within the appointed bounds of maintaining order. In contrast, when the conquistadores got to Peru they found a considerable accumulation of wealth and a corresponding accumulation of political power.

A comparison between the early American political establishment and the present one brings out the point; when in 1789 the economy of the country was largely agricultural and its total wealth was measured in millions, the scope of political authority was sharply delimited; its interventions increased in number and in extent as the productive energy of the people expanded, and now that the wealth of the nation is measured in many billions the hand of authority is felt in every private endeavor. Its interventionary powers are in proportion to its expropriation of one third of all that is produced.

When the nature of political power is put under the microscope of analysis, its incorrigible penchant for predation becomes understandable. For then one sees that political power is not "in the nature of things" but in the nature of man. It is not, like the force of gravity, self-operating and inexorable, but is an expedient devised by man to facilitate his urge for acquiring satisfactions with the least expenditure of labor. In essence, political power is the physical power, or the threat of it, that one man or a group of men may bring to bear on other men to affect behavior. It may originate in a body of social sanctions, but it is hardly political power until these sanctions are implemented with a police force. In any case, it is exercised by human beings and therefore must be related to the all-pervasive law of human action, the drive to get the most for the least.

Since all human beings are dominated by this inner drive, political power is always subject to competition, and oneman domination of the group is possible only when the group is small enough for one man to intimidate. In a real sense, there cannot be an absolute monarch of a nation; political power must have a base broad enough to support the pinnacle, and rulership which seems to be identified with one man s will is in fact exercised by an oligarchy or a bureaucracy. Political power must have allies, men who support it because it is to their interest to support it. William of Normandy consolidated his conquest of England by dividing its land among his favorites, so that they could live well on the produce of vassals and serfs. For a similar economic reason the politicians of the nineteenth century bequeathed an empire to the railroad barons of America; in both cases the beneficiaries of political power were won over to its support.

It is this need of a broad base that accounts for the predatory practices of political institutions. The crown rests uneasily on the royal brow until it is held firmly in position by the loyalty of subjects who partake or hope to partake of the substantial privileges at his disposal; and an elected official likewise needs the votes or campaign contributions of constituents who expect to profit by his elevation to power. What manner of fare can he possibly spread before them? Only what he can extract from the larder of production. He has nothing else.

The advent of popular suffrage did not change the nature of political power nor affect its practices. The doctrine on which suffrage rests is that sovereignty—which is protocol for power—resides in the voters, as a permanent possession, and that they merely loan it for a time to their selected rulers. Upon analysis the doctrine boils down to the idea that each voter holds in his hands on election day a small piece of the power that once centered in a king. But, even as the king thought of power in terms of his prerogatives and perquisites, so the voter, in casting his ballot, is influenced by his material condition or expectation of improvement. He assumes that his personal economy is tied in with the political power of distribution, not with his own productive capacity, and the assumption seems valid enough when he observes that some of his fellow voters do well at the public trough. Yet, his minuscule piece of power is by itself unable to push him into a favorable position, especially as it is in competition with millions of others of like value. It is necessary for him to add his vote to many others so that the total will bulk large in the sovereign fifty-one percent. Thus comes the pressure-group system of utilizing political power for acquiring pecuniary advantages.

But what is the profit in rulership? What does the wielder of political power—also a human—hope to gain from the bargain he makes with those who put the scepter in his hands? That depends on the values of the individual politician, but taking into consideration the breed as a whole, the desires that drive them to seek office are exactly those that motivated Charlemagne: the perquisites and prerogatives attendant thereto. What else can one derive from political labors? Putting aside the perquisites, including the crude bribe and the more sophisticated and legal methods of participating directly or indirectly in the economic advantages the politician grants his favorites, he measures his gain in the satisfaction of a desire that is often stronger than the yearning for creature comforts. Just as some people find more pleasure in music than in food, more satisfaction in climbing a high mountain than in easy living, so do others find their *summum bonum* in the pomp and circumstance of political life or in the sense of self-importance that the exercise of power stimulates. It is an ego profit that one derives from the making and administration of rules that others must obey, and with many of us this is of inestimable value. Otherwise, how account for the unseemly strife for office that men with pretensions to character engage in? "Long live the king" is the upholstery of the throne.

So, the predatory political institution that emerges when Society acquires a competence is compounded of vanity and cupidity.

But there must be some means of restraining Cain from going after Abel's hide and property, lest human fife go the way of the dinosaur. There cannot be a Society until there is a market place, and there cannot be a market place until security of possession is assured. Without that assurance the individual will not strive to improve his circumstances and production will drop to the level of mere subsistence; man will be little better than an animal, a status against which his primordial compulsions revolt. It is for that reason that he sets up a machinery for the protection of life and property, even against himself, a machinery to which he gives the name of Government.

"To secure these [inalienable] rights [to life, liberty and the pursuit of happiness]," says the best phrasing of the subject, "governments are instituted among men." It follows that if there were some way of securing these rights without Government, men would not institute it. And it also follows that when Government employs its monopoly of coercion for purposes which violate these rights it ceases to be Government. It is some other kind of concern, even as a merchantman that turns to piracy cannot be classified as a merchantman. So that, when the committee in charge of the power of compulsion use it to confiscate property they cannot lay claim to the name of Government. It is a corruption, and its name is the State.

CHAPTER 10

A State Is Born

"IN THOSE DAYS," we are told in Judges 17:6, "there was no king in Israel, but every man did that which was right in his own eyes."

To be able to do that which is right in one's own eyes is to be free, and freedom was the way of life among the Israelites before the coming of the kings. Yet, they were not without Government, they were not lacking in those social controls that are the essence of Government. The economy of the tribesmen demanded of the individual that he adjust himself to cooperative and regularized procedures; a man who indulged his caprice when the tribe was on the march in search of grazing land would be courting disaster; it was a case of hold together or die.. Tradition supplemented necessity in the orderly arrangement of life, for the tradition grew out of experience by the trial-and-error method and had proved itself beneficial. The laws of custom were sanctified because violation of them carried its own penalties, not only to the individual but also to the group. It was a conservative society; adherence to proven principles was the only way by which the pursuit of happiness could be furthered. That which was "right" in the tribesman's eyes was "right" by custom, tradition, and the laws of Yahweh, to the enumeration of which the Old Testament, before the Book of Joshua, devotes much space. Freedom is not license.

Nor was there lack of leadership before the coming of the kings. Someone had to plan strategy and improvise tactics for the wars the tribesmen engaged in during their march to the Promised Land, and someone had to adjudicate disputes so as to prevent the chaos of internecine struggles. So came the Judges, men esteemed for their wisdom and integrity, the "sports" provided by nature for the instruction of the rank and file. The evidence leads to the conclusion that these Judges ruled by natural selection and common consent, much like the chiefs of American Indian tribes. It was agreed that the authority of the Judges was sanctified by God, but the proof of their anointment was the manner in which they exercised authority. They were leaders by virtue of their proven gift of leadership.

The significant feature of the rule of the Judges is that it lacked the power of coercion. "Every man did that which was right in his own eyes" meant that no man was compelled to do otherwise; and since "in those days there was no king in Israel" it must be presumed that there was no constabulary to enforce rules of behavior. The sole enforcement agency upon which the authority of the Judges rested was public opinion. "So said Yahweh" had the force of "so say we all."

According to one computation this kind of Government lasted about four centuries—a period, incidentally, comparable to the duration of the Roman republic. The manner of its termination is recorded in the Book of Samuel, where it is told that the elders of the tribes came to the last of the Judges and demanded that he set a king over them.

The background of this agitation for a basic constitutional reform is worth noting. The nomads had by this time settled down in the hills surrounding Canaan; sheepherding was giving way to agriculture; land tenure had achieved an importance it did not have during the migrations; trading, capital accumulations, and financial transactions had entered their way of life. Their economy had changed. Their new outlook on life was colored by the vision of great wealth in the valleys; there the pomp and circumstance of Baal worship in glittering temples compared favorably in their eyes with the austerity that Yahweh imposed on them, and there all manner of private and public problems were settled out of hand by omniscient and omnipotent royal establishments, relieving the populace of rigorous self-discipline. It looked good.

The immediate occasion for the revolutionary demand was what we would today call an emergency. In fact, there were two emergencies. In foreign affairs things were going badly for Israel; the Philistines had not only beaten them roundly in battle but had also made off with the sacred ark of the covenant. On the domestic front, they had lost faith in their leadership; the two sons of Samuel, whom he had appointed as assistants, did not live up to the high standards of their office; they had "turned aside after lucre, and took bribes and perverted judgment."

Samuel seems to have been a political scientist of the first water, all the more remarkable in that he had no books to go by but was guided only by his observation of kingship in operation. So that, when the elders said "make us a king to judge us like all the nations," he was displeased. The story says that he took the matter up with Yahweh, who assured him that nothing could be done about saving the Israelites from themselves, since they had given up on first principles. It was because they had foresaken the rigorous tradition of their forefathers, with its insistence on self-reliance and personal integrity, that they had lost the victorious touch which carried them from Egypt to the outskirts of the Promised Land; the breakdown of the Judge system could be traced to the same lack of self-discipline. Therefore, said Yahweh, give them what they ask for, but as a parting shot you might "shew them the manner of the king that shall rule over them"; and tell them also that when they realize their mistake it will be too late to regain freedom: "The Lord will not hear you in that day." This is an interesting comment, seeming to stress the point that when a people put their faith in a State, rather than themselves, there is no way for them to remove the noose from their necks.

So Samuel outlined the order of things under a king. First, there will be conscription, replacing the system of voluntarism which had served the tribesmen well throughout their peregrinations, and the conscription will not be confined to military service but will include service in the king's household; what's more, women too will be subject to involuntary servitude. Then, "he will appoint him captains over thousands and captains over fifties." The term "captain" is ambiguous, referring sometimes to men of war, sometimes to what we would call a nobility, sometimes (by the kind of work assigned to them) to bureaucrats; it was in the reigns of David and Solomon that "captain" took on a variety of meanings. And, continued Samuel, the king will take from you the best of your lands "and give them to his officers and to his servants," thus establishing a landed aristocracy, which the laws of Moses clearly forbade. What's more, for the upkeep of his establishment "he will take a tenth of your seed, and of your vineyards"; apparently, compulsory taxation was new among the Israelites. To top it all off, "ye shall be his servants."

But the elders were obdurate in their demand for political authority. One could go behind the returns and make out a case against these revolutionists: perhaps they constituted a newly arisen landowning class and hoped to solidify their position under a kingship. More likely, fear had entered their hearts, as is usually the case when a people accustomed to success are faced with adversity, and they were quite willing to swap freedom for the promise of subservient security. The search for a demigod is inherent in the human makeup; fear of the problems of life tends to weaken self-reliance and to encourage belief in a deliverer. Faith in political power is a comfortable flight from reality.

In any event, Samuel anointed Saul. From the very beginning of the royal establishment the troubles of Israel multiplied. There was the usual spate of wars with the Philistines, with varying degrees of success; internal dissension, heretofore rare in the experience of the tribesmen, became common. Some followed Saul, others revolted against his rule; more exactly, they resisted the establishment of those institutions which Samuel had warned them would come with a king. But, as Samuel said, there was no way of regaining freedom once the State had made its appearance, and the Judge was soon on the lookout for a new deliverer. He sought out David, but it is significant that the new king, though anointed by Samuel, had to fight his way to power; he came to the throne on the wings of what we would call a revolution. The struggle for power, embellished with moral platitudes and social-sounding whereases, had seeped into the Israelite mores.

There is a story within the story of David's accession that is indeed a lesson in political science. The story is that a young soldier who brought David the news of Saul's death—hoping that this would be pleasing to David, whose life Saul had been after—confessed that he had had a part in dispatching the king, and for his pains David had the soldier put to death. His reason for the execution was that the soldier had defiled the office of kingship; it was a crime for an individual citizen to lay hands on the anointed. It is the way of political power to acquire a suprapersonal quality and to become in itself, regardless of the person who wields it, a shrine for public worship. Even though the incumbent proves himself unworthy, divinity doth hedge his office; it is a form of animism, by which the wielder of power is relieved of responsibility for the consequences of his use of that power. In modern times we are quick to "throw the rascals out," but it never occurs to us that rascality is imbedded in the office or that the power invested in it can make a rascal of an honest man.

Though the people of Israel had asked for a king, the spirit of freedom did not depart from them immediately upon the granting of their wish, and Saul never really set the kingship on a solid basis. It takes time for the myth of authority to gain general acceptance. David, the second king, did better, for he had forty years in which to get the tribesmen in line with the new institution; a second generation had come to maturity during his reign, and to them the exploits of royalty were "modern," real and vibrant, while the freedom of their forefathers sank into the limbo of a fairy tale. Even so, something of the past hung on, and David had to contend with frequent insurrections and, at the end, with a war of succession. He did succeed, as we learn from the Second Book of Samuel, in setting up the necessary framework for the functioning of a successful State, that is, in surrounding the king-ship with a supporting caste of "mighty men," analogous to what we would today call a privileged class, and with a group of efficient "servants" whose functions corresponded with those of latter-day bureaucrats. In that way he facilitated the consolidation of power under Solomon.

The Saul-David-Solomon story is illustrative of the gestation of the State. At first, an aspiring chieftain fights his way to ascendancy as a lone wolf, knocking off rivals, and concentrates in himself all the power he can lay his hands on. This method has merit only insofar as the area of his sovereignty is limited to personal supervision. But it proves to be quite inefficacious, and moreover quite precarious. As his quest for power reaches beyond his purview, as it always does, he finds it necessary to delegate some of his power to and share his prerogatives with a supporting oligarchy—military, ecclesiastical (or intellectual) and, in time, commercial or industrial groups which lend themselves to his purpose in return for the special privileges he grants them. They serve as a moat to his castle. In addition to these favored blocs he must surround his citadel with a class of well-paid "servants" skilled in taking care of the details of sovereignty so that it can function with the least amount of friction.

The State is not, as many political scientists would make it, an inanimate thing; it consists of people, human beings, each of whom operates under an inner compulsion to get the most out of life with the least expenditure of labor. They differ from other human beings only in the fact that they have chosen (because they believe it to be easier) the political or predatory means of satisfying their desires rather than the economic or productive means. The fiction that the State is an impersonal institution, something Society constructs for its own benefit, serves to hide, even from its members, the nature of its composition. Yet, if it were not for the economic advantages it grants to favored blocs, and if it were not for the emoluments and honorifics of political position, there would be no State. The State are people.

The wisdom of Solomon was demonstrated in his capacity for consolidating State power. In the first place, the underpinning of his reign was soundly constructed, for we are told that his captains and his princes and his priests and servants, the privileged classes, "lacked nothing." He bought off possible opposition. Then, he avoided to a considerable degree the costly and disruptive wars of his predecessors, and resorted to diplomatic bribery to bring under his sway the petty and potentially troublesome kings on the perimeter of his domain. His principal concern was in the management of internal affairs, in getting a good hold on his people by embellishing the myth of authority. The temple he built was a stroke of political genius, for it covered the kingship with an aura of omnipotence; so did the walled cities and the navy he built. These were make-work programs, to be sure, but they brought him much public acclaim and accomplished the primary political purpose, that of giving the State the character of a doer of great social things. This is the prerequisite of maintaining power over the people.

As for his method of financing these public works projects, there is nothing to instruct us in the story of his reign, except that he did employ slaves. (This form of exploitation was applicable under Hebrew law to aliens only.) There is also a hint that he exacted tribute from neighboring princes. But, as to taxation, we learn nothing until we come to 2 Chronicles (Chapter 10), which deals with the installation of his son Rehoboam. There it is told that "all Israel" pleaded with the new king thus: "Thy father made our yoke grievous; now therefore ease thou the grievous servitude of thy father, and the heavy yoke that he put on us, and we will serve thee."

It was, then, by heavy taxes that the State of Israel attained the apex of its glory under Solomon. Its opulence reflected the poverty of the people. And so it must be. Society, it should be kept in mind, is a group of people who cooperate with one another in order that they may severally and individually improve their circumstances, and the techniques by which Society achieves its purpose are production and exchange. There is no other way by which Society can thrive. Whatever deprives the members of Society of the fruits of their labors is a deterrent of the human purpose that brought them together; it is a desocializing force. And among the devices that men have invented to defeat the ends of Society none is more devastating than compulsory taxation, because it is a constant drain on their property, tending to increase as they show more and more enterprise. The State, on the other hand, thrives on what it can exact of Society; its temples are built with taxes, its bureaucracy or enforcement agency grows in size and arrogance by the same means, and it is with taxes that the State buys the support of those who might otherwise turn against it. The more taxes the richer the State, the poorer the people; the more taxes the stronger the State, the weaker the people; the interests of the two institutions are diametrically in opposition. Resistance to the State diminishes in the degree of its confiscations, and ultimately, when the tax load becomes a yoke, subservience to the State becomes the necessary condition of living.

The designation of taxation as a yoke is a nice piece of biblical directness. A yoke is worn by an ox, a beast of burden, which by nature is incapable of claiming a property right in the products of its labors. It follows that when a human being is deprived of that right his status approximates that of an ox, and if taxation takes all he produces beyond that needed to sustain life (the wages of an ox), it can rightly be called a yoke. The Israelites who pleaded with Rehoboam to lower the tax load which Solomon (the State) had put on them were quite literal.

The story goes on to say that Rehoboam rejected the plea of "all Israel," that he in fact promised them an increase in taxes. Then it tells of a revolt against taxes by the people of Judah, a political subdivision that periodically rejected the suzerainty of Jerusalem: when Hadoram, Rehoboam's chief collector of tribute, made his rounds among them they "stoned him with stones, that he died." The incident points up another lesson in political science, namely, that the State never achieves complete ascendancy over Society (if it did, Society would disintegrate and the State would collapse from lack of nutrition) and that there are always critics and rebels. There were many kings after Solomon in Israel, and all were plagued with prophets who called upon the people to return to first principles. In 2 Chronicles it says: "Israel rebelled against the house of David unto this day."

CHAPTER 11

"Social Services"

THE STATE consists of a number of people who, having somehow got hold of it, make use of the machinery of coercion to the end that they might pursue their version of happiness without respect to the discipline of the market place. They batten on Society. Taking into consideration the paraphernalia of coercion—laws, propaganda, and the police—the State might be called an institution; but at bottom it is a gang of people. The character of the State is more evident when the gang is an alien group, a conquering horde or imperialistic power, or where a distinct social class, a nobility, rides herd; then again, as under communism, where a self-anointed and self-appointed group devote themselves to the use of power. Obscurantism sets in and disguises the character of the State when the personnel of rulership is subject to periodic change, and particularly when the oligarchy convinces both itself and Society that it serves a noble purpose. It is in the phrase "social service" that the true character of the State is lost.

There are services which are indeed social, for without them there could not be a Society. The cobbler is a social servicer because he shoes people. So is the manufacturer of toothpicks or the doctor or the entertainer, or any person who devotes himself to satisfying human desires. Whether anyone is a social servicer is determined by Society, by those who willingly give up to him their possessions to avail themselves of his offerings. The more successful he is the more social he is, for his success records the quality and quantity of satisfactions he has rendered to others.

But the "social services" with which the State occupies itself are quite different in character from those that Society designates as services in the market place. They are enterprises which have nothing at all to do with the market place, are not subject to competitive conditions, do not exist because Society has chosen them to exist, and would not exist but for the power of political management to impose them on Society. Society is compelled to keep them going. Whether they are services or not is determined by the dictum of the State. Since the State is possessed of a monopoly of coercion, and has no other competence, the "services" it presumes to render cannot be subjected to any other judgment. But, though coercion is its own justification, the acceptance of it by Society calls for moral support; and so it is said that there are some services which can best be performed collectively and these are called "social."

What can be done collectively that cannot be done without the use of force? What are "social services"? The category varies with the incidence of power. In one State the operation of a railroad comes under that heading, in another this is held to be a private business. Insurance was once a service rendered by specialists to those who availed them-selves of it; now the field is being invaded and promises to be preempted by the State. Even in the same State the definition of "social services" undergoes change by force of law, as when the United States outlawed the delivery of mail by anybody but itself. The reason for this is plain: each activity that the State takes unto itself reduces the scope of social activity, adds to its personnel, and improves its position vis-à-vis Society. That is, its power increases in proportion to the number of "social services" it engages in. The process of acquisition is self-accelerating. In a highly integrated Society, where specialization is rife and each specialization impinges on another, so that none can stand up alone, the invasion of the market place by the State in one field soon brings it into contact with another, so that it is pushed by the logic of necessity into designating more and more occupations as "social" in character. Once started on this process of preemption the State cannot, if it would, contain itself; it must go on. Eventually it must abolish the market-place technique entirely; everything that man would do for himself to better his circumstances is the proper sphere of political power. Thus, the ideal of "social services" is the complete State, or communism.

Whenever the State appropriates or engages in a field of economic activity it either monopolizes it outright or surrounds it with conditions that are peculiar and advantageous unto itself, so that private operators in that field are put to flight. In the first place, the State does not tax itself and thus is relieved of a cost its competitors must bear. It is under no necessity so to manage its business that its income shall meet its expenses, for it can make up for losses by taxation. In the second place, the bookkeeping of the State is a meaningless invention of its own. Competition with the State, even when it is permitted, becomes impossible. Indeed, the State knows that it is unable to meet the performance of private business and therefore refuses to face the test of the market place. Its interest is not in rendering service but in expanding its power over Society. What are called "social services" are merely means for such expansion.

And yet, the idea of "social services" had a sound beginning. As usual, the taproot of the idea is to be found in man's search for a better life. In the days when he was organizing a Society, even as he thought of a

Government to keep things on an even keel, so he thought of other devices to make life more livable. Experience had taught him that his accumulations of labor products could be wiped out by the accident of fire. His neighbors were under the same apprehension. The upshot of this common concern was a volunteer fire department; each member of the community subjected himself to the occasional need for his services as a fire fighter because in so doing he served his own interest; in helping to save his neighbor's property he was buying protection for his own. Then there was the matter of roads, building them, keeping them open to use, repairing them. Since without roads there could be no communication between neighbors or between the various specialists offering services, a few days a year devoted to this work was not too high a price to pay for the benefits received. If there were children in the community, their educational needs were taken care of by a volunteer who had some competence for teaching. In short, voluntarism took care of a need that had not yet grown important enough to engage the services of a full-time specialist.

These services have a valid claim on the name "social." They are specializations that favor all the citizenry and yet are not identified with their separate endeavors. Thus, while the butcher, the baker, and the candlestick maker can the better ply their trades where there are thoroughfares leading to their shops, these thoroughfares are equally conveniences for the housewives who patronize them. If one of these merchants closes up shop, another will take his place if needed; if the thoroughfare is destroyed, the entire community suffers. The maintenance of the street is a social service just as an elevator in a tall building is a service for all the tenants, even though they have nothing else in common. And so with a fire department, a sanitation system, a water supply.

The part-time volunteer social servicer was outmoded by the needs of a growing population. Specialists had to take over, and specialists have to be paid. But specialists do not have to have police power to perform their services. Authority does not build waterworks, put out fires, or keep streets in repair; engineers, trained workmen, and machines do these jobs, and the only part authority can possibly take in the operation is to collect money from the citizenry and pay the bills. Yet, such is the innate characteristic of political power to enlarge upon its scope that these services are made functions of the oligarchy; the workmen who perform the work are designated "civil servants," are enrolled in the army of the State, and thus acquire a vested interest in its perpetuation and in the enlargement of its powers.

The putting out of fires could very well be entrusted to insurance companies, which have a vital interest in doing the job efficiently and at the least cost. A street-cleaning concern working under contract and hoping for renewal would be compelled by competition to do the work well and within the price agreed upon; there would be no making up a deficit by extra drafts on the taxpaying public. If a telephone company can operate efficiently and meet its obligations, including taxes, so could a private post-office system. In short, there is no service required by Society that is in any way improved by its politicalization, and that could not be better done if it were subjected to competitive conditions. The only reason for the political operation of these services is to give the State (and there is a State in every city) the semblance of a competence it does not have, so that its accumulation of power may appear to be socially beneficial.

State power is in direct proportion to State income. The more money the State has to do with, the more it will do; it is incapable of inhibiting its passion for power. A tax is a compulsory transfer of property from the producer to the ruler, and with the transfer goes the privilege of disposition. Even though the disposition of tax funds is circumscribed by law, it is still the State, not the original owner, who makes decisions. The higher the tax the narrower the scope of the producer's choices, and if all his earnings are taken from him—the Communist's program—he becomes completely dependent on the will of the legalized spender, even in the manner of how he shall live. Thus, the freedom of the individual is commensurate with the amount of his property he is able to dispose of, as he sees fit, and the power of the State is commensurate with its confiscations. And this is so even if the confiscated property is spent in ways that, according to the State, redound to his benefit. A well-kept slave is still a slave.

Nevertheless, there are these over-all or common services that enable a Society to grow both in size and in productivity, and these must be paid for. It is a poor environment, not attractive as a place to live in, and therefore not conducive to enterprise, where rivers of mud must do for streets, the outhouse is the only sanitation system, the well is the source of water supply. There is no question as to that. The only question is whether there is any means of paying for the services needed for growth other than taxation. Perhaps they can pay their own way, even as the elevator and the heating system in a large building are self-supporting. When we follow the growth of a prairie spot into a large city, step by step, we see that inherent in this development there is a source of revenue comparable to the services which make it possible.

To the first pioneer, before there is a Society, the only consideration in the selection of a site to work on is the wages this particular piece of land will yield him for his labors. To him, this is the "best" land. There is plenty of this land around, and the second, third, and other immigrants are likewise concerned only with productivity. In due time, the influx exhausts the best land, and newcomers are compelled to work the second best. A differential in desirability has arisen because of scarcity. The best is better than the second best because the same amount of labor will yield more, and if the newcomers wish to work the better locations they will offer the first occupiers a premium for the privilege. They will offer to pay rent. All things considered, the rent they will offer to pay will be equal to the differential in yield.

So far, fertility determines the rent of land. But, when the population increases to the point where specialization and trade set in, a differential in desirability of locations arises that has no relation to crops. The blacksmith does not need an acre to ply his trade, only a lot, and the doctor needs even less space. On minute fractions of a farm, men produce goods and render services that are in considerable demand, and specialists in these lines bid high for these fractions. Their bidding is the result of crowding, and the crowding in turn is due to the concentration of population in the area of these sites. Thus comes Main Street, with its general store, its hotel, its theater, and its library.

Main Street is not merely a thoroughfare. Here one can enjoy the pleasures of social life, here one can produce things of value, here one can put one's savings to productive use. It is more than a location, it is an opportunity to render and to receive services. The opportunity is sought after, and the intensity of desire for sites on Main Street fixes rental value. The bids do not represent a charge on the occupier's income, wages on his labor, or interest on his investment, but rather measure the opportunity which the desired spot will give him to work and to invest his capital. It is for the opportunity that he is willing to pay a share of the production made possible by the location. The opportunity costs him nothing, because if he did not apply his skills and his capital there, if he were compelled to locate "off the beaten track," his returns would be commensurately less. If he has rare skill to offer, like singing, it is necessary that he display it here, for elsewhere customers would be few. If he has much capital to invest, he puts up his building or his haberdashery shop at this center of population because on the prairie his capital would be unproductive. He pays for the opportunity to produce out of the production the site makes possible, not out of his earnings. In point of fact, the rent comes in by the front door.

Main Street—used here as a symbol of the market economy—is made possible by population. Population concentrates in the locality, in the first place, because the locality promises a return on invested labor and capital, because it has good land, a harbor, a mine or, eventually, a factory. That is the first magnet for people. But, since men do not live by bread alone, the wages earned in the locality begin clamoring for services that only Main Street can provide, and as wages increase so does the clamoring. Among the services demanded are those that are conducive to better living, security from fire hazards, sanitary conditions, better streets, a water supply. And as these aids to better living appear, the place becomes attractive to more people, and the bidding for locations becomes more lively. The rental values of these locations increase. But so do the productive possibilities. Rent is the reflection of density and productivity of population. Procreation and immigration are only partial boosters of rent; even more important are the wealth-producing capacities and facilities of these occupiers of sites.

The cause-and-effect relationship between rent and population productivity suggests that rent is a proper fund to apply to those services that cannot be ascribed to the efforts of individual producers, but which are necessary to all of them. This is the device first suggested by the French Physiocrats in the eighteenth century and later advocated by Henry George under the name of the "single tax." As a fiscal measure it commends itself on several grounds. In the first place, it is really not a tax, because the element of coercion is absent from the collection of rent. Rent has to be paid even as one must pay for the services of a doctor or the acquisition of any economic good. It is a price paid for the exclusive use of a desirable site and is determined by free competition. As in the case of a necktie or a ticket to the circus, the price is set by voluntary bidders; the owner of the site has nothing to do with establishing its rental value. The only question involved is whether it is in the best interests of Society, which creates this rental value, that it be paid to the owner or to the public treasury to defray the costs of the social services. To the occupier the matter is of no consequence; he does not care whether the recipient of the rent is an idiot, a genius, a corporation, or the community.

Then, there is the matter of equity. Since the social services attract population and are therefore conducive to greater production, which in turn increases rent, it would seem that the cost of maintaining them is a proper charge against rent. It can be argued that rent rises in proportion to the availability of services provided by private specialists, such as factories, doctors, railroads, entertainers, and merchants. But these are the concomitants of population density, which is directly influenced by the conditions which make the locality a desirable place to live in. It may be possible to earn as much money wages for a given amount of labor in a mining camp, where no social services are available, but a mining camp is a poor place to spend one's life in. The density and productivity of population is the primary cause of rent, but contributory to density and productivity are the social services provided in the locality. Hence, it seems equitable that this rent be used to defray the costs.

Finally, there is the obvious improvement in the abundance of the market place if taxes were abolished, if production were relieved of the cost of providing social services. A tax is a levy on earnings; it is a draft on the wages that would, if left with the earner, result in effective demand for goods and services. They are made poorer by the levy. On the other hand, rent is not a charge against production but is merely payment for the opportunity to produce. The merchant who says that he does not care what the rent of his location is so long as he can do the business there, is an excellent economist; he knows that he is not out of pocket for the rent he pays, that this payment is merely a yardstick of the volume of sales made possible at that location. If he sets up shop in a less traveled area, he will pay less rent, but he will also do less business. And he knows that the price he must charge for his merchandise is determined by competition, not by the rent he pays. Unlike a tax, which must be added to the price of the merchandise and absorbed by the consumer, rent is absorbed in commercial transactions; it cannot be passed on to the consumer.

For all that, the "single tax" does not come to grips with the basic malaise of Society, which is the tendency of political power to encroach on freedom. It is true that Henry George faced this fact, but, like all advocates of reform, his inclination to blow up his proposal into a panacea led him to pass encroachment over as an inconsequential matter that would automatically correct itself. He argued that the prosperity resulting from the abolition of taxes would offer emoluments in private enterprise that politics could not match, and that only those who had achieved a competence would enter political life for the glory of public service. But the argument does not accord with the facts of history, nor does it take into account the ineluctible urge in political life for more and more power. The power complex is not to be cured by a fiscal reform. Even as taxes are used to accumulate power, so could the rent of land. It has been estimated that rent in a highly productive country, like the United States, is a larger sum than its taxes, and if this is so its diversion to the State would make that institution stronger and more arbitrary than it is now. It could use the rent fund to take over an industry, such as the steel mills, by the simple device of declaring it a "social service." In a "democracy," how many votes could be bought with rent?

The best that can be said for the use of rent to defray the cost of social services, in lieu of taxes, is that the plan might work well in a small community. But that is so not because of the inherent virtue of the plan but because in a small community political power is more immediately responsive to social power, and any attempt to make use of the rent fund for political purposes would meet with the quick disapproval of the neighbors; that, however, is also true when taxes are misused in a small political unit. Hence, for all the merits of the "single tax," it does not meet the antisocial problems resulting from political institutions, the cure for which is the decentralization of power, the keeping of the politician within the purview of the people whose money he handles. Which is another subject.

CHAPTER 12

The Profit of Reform

THERE IS THIS to be said in behalf of avowed and doctrinaire socialists, that their faith in the State is sublime. To them, the institution of political power is the unerring shepherd of the flock, the guide to the Good Society; it is also the antidote for all evil, the maker of abundance, the embodiment of justice, the sublimation of human aspirations. That they believe. To be sure, they affect an elaborate rationalism, something they call dialectical materialism, which in turn rests on a verbal agglomeration known as Marxian economics. Logic and fact without end have been applied to these notions to prove that they are only notions. But all this cerebration has turned out to be sheer waste of effort as far as influencing the true worshipers is concerned. They still believe. One cannot help but marvel at, and admire, their devotional integrity.

The religion of socialism will come into its own, its devotees maintain, only when the devil worship of capitalism is done in. Until that happy day the State will suffer from imperfections, but these imperfections are not inherent in the State; they are merely malignant capitalistic growths that will easily succumb to socialistic surgery. The true glory of the State will become evident when the anointed priesthood are enthroned in its temples (by force, if necessary), who will then proceed to give daily demonstrations of its miraculous omniscience, to say nothing of its omnipotence. Meanwhile, it is the duty of the faithful to build up the power of the State, to reduce the area of expression for baneful and heretical individualistic thought, so that when resistance to the State becomes fatuous there will be none competent to administer its grandeur properly except the learned bishops of the church.

For that reason we find socialists aligned with nonbelievers in the prosecution of reforms which promise to improve the power of the State. But they are not reformers. Their interest in reform stems from expediency; the reform is simply a tactical maneuver that fits in with their grand strategy.

The reformer is also a dedicated person, but the object of his devotion is not a completely revised political order, only a specific improvement in the going one. His enthusiasm may read panacea possibilities into his proposal, but he is primarily interested in correcting a specific evil, real or imaginary. He asks for a law, with necessary sanctions, that will compel people to change their wicked habits, that will effect social justice, that will abolish scarcities and create abundances, that will even harness wayward nature. Whatever it is that he hopes to achieve, his espousal is characterized by a strong sense of morality and the conviction that political power is the corrective moral instrument.

Whether or not the administration of the law, if the reformer succeeds in having it enacted, does produce the results he believed it would, or makes for evils worse than the one he sought to correct, the net effect is to increase political power, to weaken social power. The residuary legatee of all reforms is the State. So that the reformer turns out to be an unwitting ally of the socialists, who really despise him for his lack of spiritual understanding.

The best-advertised reform in all history was that effected by Joseph the Provider. The Bible tells us that the whole thing started with a dream, which is quite characteristic, because all reforms germinate in fantasy. In this case, the evil that Joseph sought to correct was an inadequacy in the ways of nature; or so the story says, although it might be that the hurt visited on the Egyptians by famine was intensified by Pharaoh's taxes; we have reason to believe that taxation, not profligacy, left little with which to tide over the depression. Joseph thought otherwise, and his remedial proposal proved quite pleasing to Pharaoh because it involved the imposition of a new levy. (Here we have the earliest known case of "taxation for social purposes.")

Joseph's reform was so sure-fire, airtight in every respect, that Pharaoh adopted it with alacrity. And, of course, he lifted the reformer right out of his seat in Potiphar's jail to the seat of prime minister. What was the result of the reform? The twenty-percent income tax which Joseph collected during the years of plenty piled up in the public treasury, as intended, but when the hungry workers asked for a return, as promised, they were informed that there was a purchase price on their confiscated property. The price, at first, was all their capital, their stock, and their lands, and when that was gone, being hungry, they sold themselves into slavery to Pharaoh. Thus, Joseph's reform did what all reforms do, it increased political power. Maybe Joseph did not intend it that way—reformers must not be blamed for the contrariness of their reforms; he was, perhaps, deficient in his knowledge of political science, from which he might have learned that the State never passes up a chance to accumulate power.

Approximately forty centuries later the farmers of America were faced with an economic disability of proportions. In this case the hurt was not caused by nature but by the law of the land. There was a great disparity between their income and their cost of living, caused by the fact that while they were compelled to accept for their product the price set in the competitive world market they were concurrently compelled to pay tariff-laden prices for their manufactured needs. Equity demanded the abolition of tariffs, but this would have weakened the power of the State, which would not do at all. So, some reformer came up with the idea that the farmer's income be augmented with taxes levied on the rest of the population (even as the income of protected manufacturers is improved by tariffs) to the indefinable point where farm income would equal farm outgo. This was called "parity." The politicians took to it not because they either understood the terms of the proposed law or foresaw its effects, but because advocacy of it promised them the preferment to which their lives were dedicated.

The bonanza promised the farmers turned out to be largely promise; since most of the farms of the country are owned on mortgage or are operated on a tenancy arrangement, a considerable portion of the subsidy goes to the mortgagees or real owners; more important, the artificial price which the State sets on crops puts them out of the world market while the domestic market is constricted by the tax-reduced purchasing power of consumers. As with all subsidies, some people do get something for nothing out of "farm relief," the rest of Society pay the bill, and the net profit is an augmentation of State power. For the reform measure, in operation, produced a multitude of unforeseen problems, each of which called for a remedial law and more enforcement agents, until at long last the farmer of America finds himself controlled, regulated, and otherwise harassed by the authorities. The dream of reform always portends a profit for Pharaoh.

When we reduce the abstraction "political power" to its operational reality, to the way it actually works, we see how it feeds on reform. Every proposal to improve man's lot by political measures calls for the enactment of a law or an official edict. The law presupposes that some people are not doing what they ought to do or are doing something that ought not to be done. Hence, the purpose of the law is to regulate human behavior. The very premise of the law is that violation or evasion will ensue from its enactment, that it will not be self-enforcing; therefore, the heart of the law is a punishment clause. No law is worth the paper it is printed on without such a clause, and no law has any effect unless it is implemented with a corps of enforcers. Therein lies the secret of the accumulation and perpetuation of political power.

Joseph's reform law was carried out by what the Bible calls "officers"—stout fellows who performed their duties with finality. Where authority is diffused and highly formalized, as in this country, the arbitrament of force is resorted to only when the subtler methods of suasion and bribery have been exhausted, methods that require the services of highly trained "officers," currently known as bureaucrats. The bureaucrats are people, not unlike the people whose direction is entrusted to their care under the law; they too are bent on getting the most out of life with the minimum of exertion, and they too adjust their thinking to the means at hand. They develop an occupational frame of mind, a bureaucratic psychology. It is *sui generis*, or becomes so after a period of inurement. The mind of the bureaucrat can be compared, and without invidious intent, with the criminal mind in that it takes its shape from the peculiarities of the trade. Like the criminal, the bureaucrat is removed from the disciplines of the market place, gaining his living not by production but by predation. There the similarity ends, because the trade of the bureaucrat is legalized and does not suffer from social disapproval; in fact, because the bureaucrat is presumed to be a "civil servant," his trade acquires an aura that neither the thief nor the producer can hope for.

The bureaucrat likes his job. The emoluments may or may not be as great as what the market place would pay for such real services as he may be able to render to Society, but the kudos which is heaped on those who exercise or represent or have access to power is of importance; his ego pay is not to be despised. But his job depends on law, not on production, and therefore his primary concern is in law, its enactment, its perpetuation, its enlargement. The more law the better; which is another way of saying that his mind is keenly attuned to the possibilities of reform. The proliferation of reforms means the proliferation of bureaucratic jobs, with a corresponding abundance in honorifics and opportunities for the ambitious. Thus, a vested interest in reform appears, developing both a class-conscious distinctness and the skills necessary to its perpetuation and advancement. The bureaucracy is an aristocracy of office; it is vital to this aristocracy that offices once established be perpetuated, even though the occasion that brought them into being is long past, and that those which cannot be kept alive be replaced by others. The vested interest sees to it that the power of the State does not diminish.

Strictly speaking, laws are made by monarchs and legislators. It was Pharaoh who proclaimed the law, not Joseph. But it was on the advice of Joseph that Pharaoh acted. In our "democratic" era, when parliaments make laws, it is the bureaucrat who phrases them, who prepares the supporting arguments (which legislators mouth), who estimates (or underestimates) the costs of operation, who sets up the machinery (jobs) to implement the laws. And when a law in operation does not effect the solution of the problem it was supposed to solve, but produces problems of its own, it is the bureaucracy that comes up with correctives. Ideologically, the bureaucracy is always "leftist" (if by that term is meant the enlargement of State power), not so much by persuasion but because of personal interest and the psychology of the trade. A bureaucrat is a socialist, or communist, because his business requires him to think like a socialist or a communist.

Once a law enters the statute books it is beyond the purview of those who made it, the legislators or the king, and becomes the special, private province of those who operate it. The more numerous and prolix the laws, the more important and the more self-sufficient are the operating specialists. No part-time legislator (whose principal concern is in getting elected) or king (preoccupied wtih enjoyment) can possibly make his way through the labyrinth of law without a guide. Thus the real governing body of the country is its practicing bureaucracy, whose prospects brighten with each reform that becomes law.

The interventionary powers of the State are in direct proportion to its revenues; it must have the wherewithal with which to do things. But the visual evidence and actuality of its powers is the bureaucracy, so that its size is a sure measure of the magnitude of these powers. To put it another way, every interventionary measure calls for an enforcing agency, since it cannot enforce itself, and the operatives of this agency must be paid—not to mention the cost of necessary appurtenances, such as offices and equipment and buildings. To what purpose would the State put its revenues if it did not have a bureaucracy to maintain? Which, in a way, is a redundancy, for the bureaucracy is the State. The expenses of the State are the expenses of the bureaucracy, just as the powers of the State are realized in the functions of the bureaucracy. It is the size and importance of this aristocracy of office that actualizes the State. Therefore, when this aristocracy puts in claims on the tax fund, it is simply taking care of its business, and when it takes up with some reform measure that will entail more expenditures, it is acting in character.

A history of reform in America would have to devote most of its pages to the last hundred years, and, if it were realistic rather than ideological in its appraisal of results, it would concentrate on the growth of bureaucracy in the last fifty. In the beginning, say from the period of colonization to the Civil War, the overpowering concern of the American people was production and accumulation; there was little interest in the possibility of improving Society by political means. The Revolution can hardly be classed as a reform, since it was spurred by an urgency to curtail political power, not to enlarge it; the expectation of the revolutionists was freedom, not favors, from the State, so that they could the better get on with their digging, manufacturing, shipping, marketing, and the pursuit of happiness. The idea of using political means to improve one's circumstances could hardly have occurred to the revolutionists because there was too little produced for political power to confiscate. Taxes were low and collection was difficult. Some British citizens and agents enjoyed what few privileges the Crown did hand out, but the privileges had little cash value and therefore aroused little envy. Reform, such as it was, was confined to moral and religious practices, but even there the authorities carried little weight because one could escape their interventions by moving into the wilderness.

After the Revolution, the new political establishment began sowing its wild oats, economically speaking. Since the Constitution, and the spirit of the people, held the power of taxation in leash, the establishment had little with which to expand its prerogatives; it was too poor to attract reform. The best it could do was to give away the vast uncharted area over which it had paper control to its favorites, including members of the State, for gambling purposes. Some people made a pretty penny out of this original giveaway, but since there was still plenty of land to be had for occupancy, use, and even gambling, the wealth thus acquired aroused little cupidity and therefore no reform movement; when loot is plentiful and liberally distributed, moralizing is out of place.

About the only reform that showed its head in the early years of the Republic was an urgency for cheap money. It started, in Massachusetts, even before the Constitution was ratified, and its proponents were, of course, the large debtor class who hoped to pay off their mortgages with printing press money. The history of money reform, from Shays' Rebellion, through Jackson's fight on the United States Bank, down to the era of wildcat banks and the Greenbackers, culminated finally in the repudiation of the gold standard by Franklin D. Roosevelt and the establishment of inflation as a national policy. It began as an attempt to get rid of private debts and ended up as a devious taxing scheme; that is, the reform redounded to the benefit of the State. And now that the State has taken inflation under its wing, the bureaucracy that "controls" it is a very busy institution, employing thousands of operatives, including learned professors of economics. Whether the debtors ever got a penny out of their cherished reform is questionable.

Another reform that loomed large in the early days was the agitation over protective tariffs, pro and con. Nothing came of it except the

Civil War and higher tariffs—and a considerable army and navy of collectors and snoopers and tariff "experts"; that is, a bureaucracy. The fact that protected industries have had a record of bankruptcy equal to that of unprotected industries indicates that the advocates of higher tariffs did not profit much by their reform. The State did.

It was not until some years after the Civil War, when three centuries of productive effort bore fruit in a general increase of wealth and leisure, that reform became a major interest in this country. During the last quarter of the nineteenth century there was a hatful of reforms from which the citizen could take his pick, and every one of them began with the premise that political power could improve the lot of man economically, socially, morally, and even culturally. There was prohibition, woman suffrage, direct election of senators, free coinage of silver, subsidies to farmers, extension of the educational system, antitrust measures, control of railroads, and what not. In the main, the redistribution of wealth stirred up the most violent enthusiasm, and most of the reforms advocated had all the earmarks of envy. The have-nots were at the haves. The reformers made no distinction between fortunes that were amassed by productive effort and fortunes that had their origin in the politically established special privileges; in fact, the reforms did not aim at the abolition of special privileges but at the establishment of more special privileges for more groups. Political power could make everyone rich.

A promising exercise in political science would be to follow each reform that became law to its ultimate conclusion; even a cursory examination supports the theory that all re-forms end up in additions to State power, and that none of them achieves the high purpose expected by its advocates. This is certainly true of the income tax, which should be called the reform of reforms because its attainment made possible a flock of reforms.

An income tax was imposed during the Civil War and was continued for half a dozen years to clean up the costs of that affair. Its abolition was vigorously opposed by those who had gotten a taste of blood, and their overpowering passion for more of it finally culminated in the Sixteenth Amendment. It was admittedly a leveling tax, the presumption being that what was taken from the pockets of the rich would somehow trickle into the pockets of the poor. But the State, as history tells us, is not concerned with the fate of the poor or the rich, its protestations to the contrary notwithstanding, but only with its own advancement. This opportunity to pick pockets could not for long be limited to a few that obviously bulged large. It was soon learned that all these pockets collectively contained less loot than the national pay envelope, and when that fact was ascertained the itching fingers of the State could not be restrained. So that the "soak the rich" tax has become a "soak the poor" tax. Most of the income of the American State is now derived from the earnings of those least able to bear the burden.

The income tax opened the floodgates of reform. It is interesting to note that while in the nineteenth century most reforms originated in the notions of dissident elements in the population, the reforms that have become law since the introduction of the income tax were instigated by bureaucrats. They had the money with which to indulge their passion for power. Certainly, the reform ideas seemed to spring from colleges, shops, and organizations, but there is evidence that they took form in the imagination of the vested interest, whose propaganda machinery gave enthusiasm for the reform a popular flavor. And so came the New Deal, which is the name given to a host of interventions called "social legislation." Each of these measures called for the establishment of another enforcement agency, more offices, buildings, and jobs. The bureaucracy did well by itself.

The net profit of reform is the accumulation of State power; the net loss is borne by Society. Out of the reforms advocated by the Gracchus brothers came the Caesars and "bread and circuses." Pericles set up a number of make-work projects and ruled for thirty years, subtly but with an iron hand. Bismarck was a reformer. Mazzini was the unwitting forerunner of Mussolini. Lenin was the archreformer of all times, in that his reforms culminated in the largest, the most arbitrary, and the most ruthless bureaucracy the world has ever known.

CHAPTER 13

The Maker of Shortages

WHENEVER AND HOWEVER the State intervenes in the affairs of men, particularly their economic pursuits, a lessening of satisfactions ensues. The consequence of political intervention is on a par with that of a raid on the market place, say by a band of robbers: a depletion of the things men live by. We are talking of consequence, not of intent. The robber band makes no pretensions to character, while the State clothes its operations with a moral purpose, such as the promotion of the "general welfare"; but in both cases the sum total of consumable or capital goods is diminished. Society has less. Since the keystone of the social structure is man's everlasting struggle to avoid shortages and to achieve abundances, the shortage-producing consequence of the State's interventions stamp it as an antisocial institution. It must be classed with the robber band, and only its loud protestations of a moral purpose, which are generally believed because skepticism is likely to bring on discomfort, prevent its being so classed.

The first item on the agenda of the State is taxation, simply because the State could not exist without it. A tax is a compulsory exaction; it is not a voluntary payment for goods received or services rendered. In ancient times, before a regularized system obfuscated it, the nature of a tax was better understood, for it frequently consisted of the lifting from the producer's premises of goods he had labored for in the expectation of enjoyment: his corn, cattle, or other accumulations. That was palpable evidence of the scarcity-producing nature of taxation. No mutation occurs when the tax is collected in the form of money; it is still part of what the producer has labored for in the hope of satisfying his desires. It is shoes, bread, entertainment.

Taxation not only robs the market place of consumable goods, which is the true measure of a nation'xss economy, but it also reduces the productive capacity of Society by its absorption of savings, or capital. It is obvious that the individual cannot save what he does not have. And since savings become investments in productive machinery, the lack of savings means a shortage of those instruments that make abundance possible. Thus, taxation deprives the consumer of immediate satisfactions and lessens the possibility of plenty in the future. In both effects, taxation is a shortage-creating institution, and that is not what men have in mind when they merge themselves into Society.

Idolators of the State are wont to counter this fact with the observation that productive effort seems to increase with an increase in taxation, inferring that the activities of the State are economically beneficial. This is equivalent to saying that men work to pay taxes and that the bigger the tax load the greater their productivity. If this were so, then the wealthiest and healthiest economy would be achieved by the State's confiscation of everything produced—which is the claim of communism. Yet the production figures that leak through from communist countries add up to economies of scarcity, to an abundance of shortages. And historians tell us that the continuing and mounting exactions of the Roman emperors caused a lack of interest in productive enterprise, so that the net income from taxes decreased and the emperors resorted to conquest and loot to replenish their coffers; when conquest proved unprofitable and production did not yield enough to pay expenses, the State collapsed.

The argument of the Statists rests on the production figures of this country, which show that the mounting tax load has been accompanied by an increase of production. But this is a coincidence, easily explainable, and not a cause-and-effect relationship. It indicates that the American tax load has not yet reached the point of diminishing returns. The two thirds of his earnings that the American is allowed to keep is still an inducement to try to maintain and better his standard of living. A man will work hard to repair the damage caused by a storm, or to replenish what the thief has taken from his safe, but this does not mean that the storm or the thief improves his economy., What he has lost by depredation or accident is a loss, not a gain. The fuel of productive energy is not taxes, but the inner compulsion of the individual to improve his lot.

Granting all that, does not the State perform services which indirectly aid in producing abundances? Does it not return to Society something of value for what it takes?

Foremost among the services which the State claims to render Society is its protection from other predatory States. This is a considerable service, to be sure. In former times, when political morals were differently phrased, the State prosecuted war with the avowed purpose of adding glory to its name by way of real-estate acquisitions, to say nothing of the ancillary purpose of bringing civilization to barbarians; Napoleon's avowed ambition was to impose on his victims the blessing of "liberty, fraternity, equality." This is out of fashion these days; wars are now waged to protect the nation from the aggressor, which is the name each side gives to the other. However, it is still *de rigueur* for the victorious State to add to its exploitable territory at the expense of the conquered. But we are not here concerned with the aims of war, nor with its causes or its avoidability; what interests us is the effect on Society's economy. Does the housewife have more in her pantry, or less, as a result of the glorious adventure? Does Society acquire shortages or abundances? What is the economic profit of the military protection afforded by the State?

Putting this economic consideration aside, there is the inescapable fact that paying homage to a foreigner goes against the grain of tradition. Until he made his accommodation to the inevitable, no decent Saxon would have any truck with his Norman overlords, and the Indians always resented the British *raj*. It is this abhorrence of rule by foreigners that makes it easier to stir up a revolt against a State so composed than against an indigenous one. Yet, on balance, are the Indians better off, economically, under their own State than when the British ruled the roost? And the Canadians, who did not emulate the Americans in getting rid of the British Crown, nevertheless enjoy a comparable standard of living. That is to say, regardless of the nationality of the State, Society has to make its way by the usual process of laying labor to raw materials, and the vaunted protection of the State neither promotes nor facilitates that process.

Since Society puts so high a value on independence from a foreign State, it should not demur at the cost of maintaining this independence. One must pay for what one wants. However, when we examine the most approved method of financing war we find that it is based on a general reluctance to foot the bill. Every war is fought with current production—there is no way of shooting off guns that have not yet been made or of feeding soldiers with food that will be raised by the next generation—and in a real sense every war is con-ducted on a pay-as-you-fight basis. But the producers of the means of war seem to put a lower value on it than do the management, for they demand receipts for what is taken from them to prosecute the war, receipts which become a claim on future production, not only as to their face value but also as to the interest: which patriotism demands; it is possible that if the State raised all the costs of war by taxes, issued no bonds or even issued only non-interest-bearing bonds, the war might be called off, which would be proof enough that Society puts little worth on its political purposes. The economic conseqence of the most approved method of financing wars is that a lien on the future production of the nation is established, and nearly always it is a permanent lien. That is, for all time to come, or as long as the State stays in business, the housewives' pantries must contribute to the cost of a nation's past "protective" wars.

But war, and the preparations for it, is attended with a charge that has nothing to do with protection and is a load that increasingly hampers Society in its search for a better life. That is the power which the State acquires during war and does not relinquish when it is over. When the enemy is at the city gates, or there is a general fear that he is coming, the individual abdicates his self-reliance and places himself unreservedly under the direction of the captain; he gives up his freedom in order to attain freedom. Or so he thinks. But it is a matter of record that what he gives up is never fully returned to him, that he must fight his own captain to get back his natural heritage. The State jealously guards the power over Society which it has acquired during a climate of fear. To prove the point, we need not review the history of ancient Rome, where a succession of protective wars ended up in the servitude of the people to the emperors; we need only list and add up the interventionary powers acquired by the American State during the wars it conducted; the sum total is a monstrous tax load, a monstrous bureaucracy, a monstrous statute book, and a popular conviction that the State (which was feared and despised in 1789) is the giver of all things good. So, then, the "protective" service rendered by the State is paid for not only with taxes but also with subservience. Society is much poorer for it.

It is when the State undertakes to manage, regulate, or control the market place, or presumes to enter it as an entrepreneur, that its capacity for causing shortages is best displayed. Necessarily, the State brings to bear in such ventures the only tool in its kit—force. It has no other equipment. Not that the bureaucracy, if they applied themselves as individuals to production, could not do as well as other individuals of equal capacity, but that as bureaucrats they feel no call to meet the conditions of the market place; they have force at their command and their business is to use that force. And force, in the political sense, is to the market place as sand is to a machine.

Let us look to a few of the State's forays into the market place which it undertakes in the interest of the "general welfare."

The encouragement of home industry by limiting or excluding competitive importations has been standard procedure with the State since time immemorial. The foreigner's wares are kept out of the home market not because he insists on offering them, but because the home market demands them. A country imports only what it wants. Hence, the tariff has the effect of restraining the primordial urge of the human being—to satisfy his desires with the least effort, at the lowest cost. It makes for scarcity, the very condition that man instinctively seeks to avoid. This is not only a result of the tariff, it is the purpose of the tariff. It is admittedly a scarcity-producing device, and as such it is antisocial. This is emphasized by the ready market which the smuggler, who always follows in the wake of a tariff, enjoys.

The State, particularly in modern times, often assumes an entrepreneurial role "for the good of Society." When it does so it invariably makes use of its monopoly of compulsion to exclude competition from the field into which it enters, or at least to make competition difficult. It admits its own incompetence—its lack of equipment for anything but the acquisition or exercise of power—by removing its operations from comparison with the performance of private entrepreneurs. It fixes its prices and its standards of performance to suit its own convenience and leaves the consumer no recourse. Indeed, as in the case of our post office, the State compels the non-consumer to pay for its upkeep; the man who never sends or receives a letter is forced through taxes to make up the operational losses of the department. These losses, deficits, are *prima facie* evidence of the department's inadequacy, which the State hastens to cover up by declaring that the deficits represent more services than the user of the post office pays for. Whether this is so or not, only competition could tell, and that the State will not allow. Under the circumstances, it is safe to conclude that whenever the State undertakes to make goods or render services for which there is a demand it does so without regard to the wishes of the consumer. That it causes shortages can be ascertained by comparison with the performance of privately operated services in comparable fields (as, for instance, the telephone service versus the post office). Making a shortage is a social disservice.

The shortage-inducing proclivity of the State is best shown when it undertakes to regulate, manage, or manipulate the market place. The occasion for such efforts is social unrest due to scarcities, caused either by the State's own interventionary measures or by some disaster, such as a drought, flood, or conflagration. Since scarcity causes a rise in price, to the discomfort of the consumer, the State, which is utterly incapable of causing the abundance that would reduce price, attempts to make use of its compulsory powers to accomplish that end. It always fails. Not only that, the measures it employs invariably cause a greater shortage.

A prime example of this is the fatuous efforts to control or fix rents. The increased cost of living space is caused by a shortage of houses. Putting aside the accidental destruction of houses, the shortage generally results from the diversion of materials and labor from the construction of houses to the production of military material. New dwellings are not produced and old ones are allowed to decay. Under the conditions the action of the market place automatically pushes up the price of space to a level some dwellers are unable to meet and causes others to do without other things in order to keep a roof over their heads. This causes dissatisfaction, which the State undertakes to assuage by peremptorily ordering house owners to hold rents at a fixed figure; incidentally, it diverts attention from the real cause for the high rents by implying or asserting that they evidence the brash cupidity of the house owners. Since the rents fixed by law are invariably lower than the cost of maintaining the properties, including the services that go with tenancy, the law in fact orders the owner to dig into his pocket to make up the deficit. That amounts to commanding him to make a present of his capital to the renter. To avoid that consequence, and to keep within the law, he cuts down on the service implied in the lease as well as on the repairs necessary for the upkeep of his property. Assuming that there is no collusion between the renter and owner to evade the law, the renter does pay less than the market price of his space, but he also gets less: less heat, less paint, less plumbing repairs, less cleanliness, less elevator services, and so on. Thus, rents are controlled on the statute books only.

Rent controls have the effect of continuing and increasing the shortage of houses which brought on the controls. For builders are reluctant to invest their capital in the construction of houses which, because of the controls, will not yield a return equal to costs or equal to what a like investment in some other line would yield. It is a well-known fact that very few houses, far fewer than are needed, have been erected in France since it instituted rigid rent controls after World War I. That is to say, the State's forays into the market place, in the interest of the "general welfare," invariably work to the disadvantage of Society.

The ingenuity of the State in taking advantage of every contingency to promote its own business, which is the accumulation of power, is illustrated in the way the American political establishment met the scarcity aggravated by its rent-control venture. Seeing that rent control did not control but rather worsened the housing shortage, and being reluctant to admit its error, it supplemented control with subsidization. It subsidized builders, it subsidized bankers who made loans to builders, and it subsidized renters. The builders overvalued the housing projects they undertook, so that the bankers would make large loans, which the State guaranteed to pay in case of default, and in that way the entrepreneurs received what they would have lost had they depended on the low-rent payments fixed by law. The difference between market rent and legal rent was made up by taxes, and the dignity of the law was upheld. One consequence of this maneuver was to put upon the taxpayer a continuing load; another, and that is most important from the State's point of view, was the establishment of a permanent bureaucracy to manage the problems that subsidized housing entails: the evaluation of loan applications, the setting up and supervision of construction standards, the checking of amortization and interest payments, the enforcement of rules and regulations for subsidized renters. In the offing is another bureaucracy for the execution of foreclosures. Society acquired taxes and the State acquired power.

This is true whenever the State presumes to regulate the market place. The rent-control business is used here as an illustration. Price control of any kind must produce scarcities and therefore cause prices to rise to still higher levels, simply because the fictitious price discourages the production of the abundance that would automatically reduce price; price control has the same effect on the output of a factory as the subsistence wage has on the output of a slave. And in an integrated economy, where each specialized field of activity impinges on and is dependent on other fields, the attempt to fix a price of one commodity compels an attempt to fix other prices; a fixed price on a cup of coffee necessitates control of the price of cream, sugar, coffee beans, transportation, and all the services involved in bringing the beverage to the consumer. Wages, the largest element of cost, must also be included in the rubric of rigidity. It is obvious that the effort to regulate distribution at the point of price must be followed by an attempt to regulate production, to the allocation of raw materials, to the fixing of production standards, to the limitation of variety—to shortages. An economy cannot long remain half free and half socialistic. As soon as Society accommodates itself to one intervention, accepts it as a necessary condition of existence, the resulting scarcity calls for a contiguous interference, which is the more easily introduced because of the antecedent adjustment.

What exactly is meant by price, wages, rent, interest? These mechanisms of the market place are self-operating, self-controlling, inanimate, and quite oblivious of human whim. They reflect what humans do, to be sure; prices rise if humans produce less and demand more; they drop when humans produce more and consume less; they do so automatically and regardless of statutes. They cannot be controlled by political power, and the State concedes that point when it includes in the price-control law a punishment clause. The punishment law is not directed at price but at men. This is the only field in which the State has any competence—the regulation of human conduct by the use of coercion. The price-control law directs the consumer not to pay more than the legal list for his satisfactions, and it instructs the producer not to accept more. If either or both of them disobey the interdict, the law says, punishment will follow. Thus, a price-control law does not aim to control price, which is beyond the jurisdiction of the State, but aims to control human behavior. And that, of course, is a denial of freedom—which is no concern of the State.

CHAPTER 14

A Matter of Degree

THE SMALL STATE can do to Society everything the large State can do, but not so much of it. The tyranny and terrorism of modern communistic overlords is of a kind with the practices of ancient Sparta, and twenty-five centuries before Mr. Roosevelt launched the New Deal, Pericles had something closely resembling it. Sparta and Athens were small aggregations, compared to their modern counterparts, and so there were fewer people to ride herd on; also, because they were less productive, there was less for the bureaucrats to lay their hands on. But the pattern of intervention and confiscation was the same. A State is a State, now as in the past, regardless of the size of its victim, and regardless of ideology affected by its management. It is always at war with Society.

The history of our own political subdivisions—states and cities—is well splattered with instances of "corruption." Our newspaper headlines and our campaign oratory periodically bear witness to the persistence of predatory practices by political management, even in our smaller communities. "Throw the rascals out" is the standard battle cry in our contests for political preferment, indicating that rascality is the regular order. But, when we dig down to the bottom of the rascality, we find some interventionary law that was ushered in with yards of moral fustian. It is the law itself that stimulates the cupidity of the official and his private accomplice. The policeman would not help himself to a banana from the peddler's pushcart if there were no law regulating the push-cart business, and schemes to evade taxes, including bribery, are the inevitable consequence of taxation. Interventionism is the stock in trade of every political establishment, and "corruption" is its corollary.

As an illustrative instance, on a rather grandiose scale, there is the case of the New York City subway system. Originally this railroad was built by entrepreneurs under a franchise granted by the "city fathers." As a condition of the grant, the fare was fixed at five cents. For a while all went well; the company rendered adequate service and paid its bills, including interest on its bonded indebtedness. As the city pulled into its orbit more and more surrounding communities, the company extended its mileage, as required, and in due time the nickel fare did not meet operational costs. The company asked for permission to increase its fare. The people-loving politicians refused the request and the "nickel fare" became a potent campaign issue. From the very beginning there were those who clamored for public ownership and operation, terming the franchise a "giveaway," but they were shouted down as socialists, the bondholders and management being most vociferous in this denunciation. But, when the company defaulted on its interest payments, and the bonds consequently shrank in value, it was the bondholders who asked the city to buy them out; they had no objection to socialism if a profit were involved. Eventually, a "reform" administration, headed by a mayor of pronounced socialistic persuasion, arranged for the purchase of the bonds at a price far beyond the open market quotation. The taxpayers, as usual, paid the bill. Shortly thereafter the subway was "taken out of politics," meaning that the fare was raised to ten and then to fifteen cents, and deficits are now the regular order. The subway system is now a city-owned monopoly, run by bureaucrats, whose prime interest is the perpetuation of their jobs, not railroading.

There was no obvious "corruption" in this operation, but it is known that speculators took a keen interest in the bonds when the prices declined to less than the physical valuation of the property, and that they sold them to the city at a handsome profit; even if no officials were involved in this piece of business (which is assuming that officials are more than human), the fact is that this venture in public railroading compelled the citizens to finance the acquisition, and continues to compel them to meet the operational losses. It was done by a city, not a national, establishment. Indeed, the City of New York has set a pattern for the nationalizing of the railroads of the country: a regulatory body, with power to fix rates and compel unprofitable operation, squeezes the business into bankruptcy, so that the owners are quite willing to sell their property to the taxpayers, and bureaucracy improves its position.

Another case. It does not occur to a small town to set up a department of "weights and measures"; social power soon rides the dishonest merchant out of business, if not out of the community. In a city like New York the same social power is present, but it does not make itself felt with the same expedition because of the multitude of possible victims. A number of complaints suggests an "issue" to the sagacious politician, and a law and a bureau of "weights and measures" come into being. The bureau, however, soon finds itself short of business; it is in competition with social power, which is far more effective in punishing dishonest practices than are the police. But an official body is never daunted by the lack of something to do; its capacity for digging up problems to solve is limited only by the funds at its disposal, and the funds are proportionate to the size and productivity of the taxable population. So, the department of "weights and measures" burgeons into an investigatory body, with power to pry into the malpractices of other political bodies (not itself) and achieves headlines by exposing a few firemen who take off-duty jobs, which is against the law, or exposing some prostitutes whom the police have overlooked. The headlines serve to vindicate the bureau and justify its costs.

These two instances of bureaucratic practice and political intervention in the largest city in the country can be matched, though not on so large a scale, by every city in the country. Where the grazing land is richer, there the politician waxes fatter. It follows therefore that the smaller the community, the more likelihood of confining officials to their legitimate business, that of keeping the peace and dispensing justice cheaply. Conversely, the larger the political unit, the more opportunity for the abuse of political power. If there were any point in working it out, this fact of political science could be reduced to a mathematical formula. More interesting and instructive is the reason for it.

Social power diminishes as political power increases, and political power expands in direct ratio to the size and wealth of the community over which legal authority has been established. To put it another way, the further removed from the purview of those whose behavior he undertakes to canalize, the more attenuated are the social restraints on the politician's proclivity. The reason for this lies in the fact that he is human; his occupation does not free him from the instincts and motivations of all men. In a small community, the prince or the councilman or the sheriff is under the constant surveillance of neighbors, and their opinion of his behavior is not without influence; either the desire to retain their good will or the fear of retribution bears on his official acts. He must live with them, just as a merchant must live with his customers, and social ostracism is too heavy a price to pay for indulging the passion for power which his position generates.

As the community grows this neighborly influence diminishes. Public affairs become too complex for the man preoccupied with the business of living, and his interest in them wanes in proportion; only when he is personally affected by political matters does he become concerned with them. Under the circumstances, the politician is more or less on his own.

A more impelling reason for the attenuation of social power is the splintering of its homogeneity as population grows; group interests replace the common interest and the politician finds himself under a variety of pressures. He is put in the way of acquiring power by the claims and ambitions of the various factions, each of which is willing to barter the common good for its own advantage. The logic of the situation compels him to lean toward those factions which because of their numerical or economic predominance are most promising for his purpose, the accumulation of power. Group pressures, rather than social sanctions, chart his course, and his problem is the selection of allies. Thus, when the king met with strong opposition from the feudal barons he made common cause, for the time being, with the proletariat of the cities, and in our "democratic" time it is standard political procedure for the aspirant to champion the cause of farmers as against the urban population, to court favor with wage earners by promising to despoil capitalists, to form alliances with ethnic, economic, social, and even criminal groups that can "deliver the vote." His release from the social sanctions of the small community makes of him an entrepreneur in power.

His business, however, cannot flourish without resources, and his resources are determined by what he can extract from producers. In the smaller community the producers, being relatively few, can scrutinize his expenditures closely and make their opposition to taxes felt. In the larger community, consisting of a number of self-centered pressure groups, this surveillance of his operations tends to disappear; people are too busy with their private affairs to pay much attention to the complexity of public affairs. The tendency then is to identify public affairs with their own interests or with the interests of the group to which they adhere. Under the circumstances, the political person is able to draw up a convincing bill of particulars which he calls the "need of social services" but which on examination becomes a list of expenditures from which various dominant groups or individuals in the community hope to improve their own circumstances. The opposition to expenditures and taxes is thus weakened, and his opportunity improves.

Every budget is a compromise of interests. Every tax bill, even in the smaller cities, contains a promise to levy with a heavier hand on one group of citizens than another, with the implied intention of favoring some of the citizenry at the expense of others. In the rhetoric of politics there is no more compelling peroration than "ability to pay"; it is compelling because it touches to the quick the very common sin of covetousness, because it appeals to the envy and jealousy that few men are rid of. To be sure, the insinuation of "ability to pay" is that the "poor" will gain something by a "soak the rich" measure; but it is a moot question whether it is the hope of gain or the prospect of bringing the more capable or fortunate down to their own level that makes the "ability to pay" formula so acceptable to the "poor." The class-struggle notion is a most convenient instrument of the State. In the end, of course, only the political establishment profits by the tax formula; its business prospers, while the business of Society, the production of goods and the rendering of services, slows down to the extent of the exactions.

The zenith of political aspirations is attained when the revenues at his command rid the politician of the restraint of social sanctions. Having the wherewithal to operate in his own sphere, he can lift himself above Society and assume the role of statesmanship; that is, he can assume a capacity for improving the "general good," as he sees it, uninhibited by the limitations and foibles of those who must pay the bill. His economic independence induces the conviction that he has acquired a consciousness of collective aspirations, which is more than the sum of the myopic and individualistic aspirations of Tom, Dick, and Harry; he knows what is for their own good better than they do. He lives in a world of his own, in which Tom, Dick, and Harry exist only as means, not as persons. Social sanctions diminish in importance as taxation increases. And taxation increases, both in amount and in variety, as population and production increase. The incidence of taxation in our own cities is illustrative; in the beginning, real-estate values bore the entire brunt; now, in our larger cities, sales taxes, pay-roll taxes, poll taxes, occupancy taxes, liquor taxes, and a variety of licenses, fees, and fines are included in the fiscal structure. Each levy rides in on the wings of "necessary government expenses," with the decision as to what are necessary expenses resting with the managing bureaucracy. Often the occasion for the levy disappears, but the levy does not; as when interest on bonds continues to be a drain on the community long after the road or the school-house which was the excuse for the issue is abandoned.

The historic urgency of political establishments for centralization, for the expansion of cities and the creation of nations, with which imperialistic ventures must be included, thus becomes meaningful. The wider the area of control the weaker the resistance of social pressures; the larger the population under control the more taxpayers to contribute to the political coffers. Centralization is the setting up of a protective distance between State and Society, of the insulation of the State from social sanctions. In a village the citizenry have an immediate influence on political behavior; when the village is incorporated into the City of Chicago, this influence tends to evaporate, particularly its impact on taxation practices.

Realization of the dangers of centralization, of the divorcement of political power from social control, gave rise to the idea of constitutionalism. A constitution undertakes to define the scope of political power, to delimit the functions the State may assume, as a condition for public support. It is a contractual agreement. But it is a matter of record that no State has long abided by the terms of the agreement; its inherent compulsion toward the acquisition of power cannot be inhibited by law. The best example of this is the life story of the American Constitution. It originated in the convention that a State is inherently incapable of containing its urge for power, and the writers not only defined and limited the scope of the new State but also provided for a system of "checks and balances" that presumably would prevent its getting out of bounds. It specifically provided that all powers not enumerated would remain with the state establishments—a clear recognition of the historic fact that political power is less virulent the nearer its wielders are to the ruled. This novel idea of states' rights, of the division of authority, was intended as a block to centralization. It had the additional effect of setting up competition between the states, so that if a political establishment undertook to put disabilities on its citizens, one could escape them by moving across the border to another state. Besides these "checks and balances" and the doctrine of *imperium in imperio*, there was the further formidable barrier to centralization in the carefully circumscribed authority to levy taxes.

Despite all this, the American State has been able to circumvent the terms of the bargain of 1789; by legal interpretation and amendment it has achieved centralization as effectively as other establishments have done by force. When we compare the intent of the "founding fathers"—and taking into consideration the social pressures that bore upon this intent—with the present state of political affairs, we can say that the original constitution has been in fact replaced by something quite different. Basically, the intent was to provide a form of political institution that would hold inviolate the immunities of person, property, and mind. The immunity of person went by the boards when military conscription was instituted as a national policy, and national policy was interpreted as an obligation to use these troops in the wars of foreign nations; this was not contemplated in 1789. The immunity of property was abolished by the Sixteenth Amendment, which, by asserting the prior lien of the State on the earnings of citizens, virtually denies them the right of private ownership; with this right gone, the right to life becomes academic. The immunity of mind has been violated by more subtle but no less effective means, which the proceeds of income taxation made available: by the establishment of a vast propaganda machine for the channeling of thought in favor of State ventures, including the distortion of facts as to its operations; by the subvention, with favors, of news-vending and opinion-influencing publications; by the subsidization of educational institutions and educators.

If the carefully constructed constitution of 1789 has not been able to contain the power-grabbing proclivities of the federal establishment, it is reasonable to conclude that no body of laws can accomplish that purpose. The key to centralization, to the consolidation of conquest, is taxation. All things considered, the Sixteenth Amendment made a shambles of the constitution of which it is ostensibly only a part. It gave the Executive branch the means of undermining the independence of Congress (which was supposed to hold it in check), for with the vast funds at its disposal it is able to purchase compliance from the legislative branch and to suppress opposition. It made possible the virtual liquidation of the autonomy of the states, first by sapping their sources of revenue and then by bringing them into line with subventions; the doctrine of states' rights has thus lost all meaning. It provided political authority with capital enough to venture into the market place as manufacturer, distributor, financier, publisher, farmer, physician, employer, to the disadvantage of private entrepreneurs. It set the State up as the largest eleemosynary institution in the history of the world. And along with all these interventionary measures came the vast bureaucracy dedicated to the perpetuation and extension of these interventions. Thus, one change in the constitution did away with its original character.

Within their respective areas, the state establishments (which are likewise under constitutional limitations) and the cities (which operate under charters from their states) have emulated the federal authority. Increases in their population were followed with correspondingly increased productivity and the appearance of abundances, which invited political raids on the market place. The proceeds of such forays, always adorned with a social purpose, enhanced political power. And social power diminished. This is a truism culled from the ages, that social power and political power are always in conflict, that the poverty of the one is the opulence of the other, that one thrives on predation, the other on production. The relationship is like that of the scales of a balance, which no parliamentary device can alter.

It follows that political authority is not containable by contract. No constitutional constriction ever invented has succeeded in keeping the political person within his appointed sphere, that of maintaining the peace within Society, of effecting equity between producers, of assuring each member that his rights shall not be invaded by another. Some other instrument of control is necessary if Society is not to be periodically swallowed up by the State.

CHAPTER 15

One Can Always Hope

IT IS NOT INCUMBENT on a diagnostician to prescribe a remedy, and it would be quackery for him to do so when he has misgivings as to its curative value. It may be that the struggle between Society and the State is inevitable; it may be in the nature of things for the struggle to continue until mutual destruction clears the ground for the emergence of a new Society, to which a new political establishment attaches itself to effect a new doom. Perhaps the malignancy is inherent in man. It would be silly to suggest that four-footed males, driven by the reproductive urge, ought to know better than engage in deathly battles over possession of females, and it is possible that the historical struggle between the social organization and the political organization is likewise meant to be.

Support for this conclusion is found in the ground we have covered.

Beginning with man—where else can we begin?—we find him impelled by an inner urge to improve his circumstances and widen his horizon; a self-generating capacity for wanting drives him from one gratification to another. Each gratification represents an expenditure of labor, which, because it produces a feeling of weariness, he finds distasteful. His inclination is to by-pass labor as much as possible, but without sacrificing his betterment. He brings to bear on this natural *modus operandi* a peculiarly human gift, the faculty of reason. (It is this faculty that suggests a possible solution of the Society-State conflict, which we will discuss later.) His reason tells him that the business of multiplying satisfactions is best pursued by cooperation with his fellow man. Thus arises Society and its techniques: specialization and exchange, capital accumulations, competition. Society is a labor-saving device, instinctively invented; it is not a contractual arrangement, any more than the family is, but like the family it germinates in the composition of man.

The market-place method yields more for less labor than individual self-sufficiency does, yet the price it always demands is labor. There is no getting away from that. Still, it is a price paid with reluctance, and out of this inner conflict between cost and desires comes the drama of organized man. The impossibility of getting something for nothing, the *summum bonum*, does not banish hope or intimidate the imagination, and in his effort to realize the dream, man frequently turns to predation: the transference of possession and enjoyment of satisfactions from producer to nonproducer. Since men work only to satisfy their desires, this transference induces a feeling of hurt, and in response to that feeling the producer sets up a protective mechanism. Under primitive conditions, he relies on his own powers of resistance to robbery, his personal strength plus such weapons as he has at his disposal. That is his Government. Since this protective occupation interferes with his primary business of producing satisfactions, and is frequently ineffective, he is quite willing to turn it over to a specialist when the size and opulence of Society call for such a service. Government provides the specialized social service of safeguarding the market place.

The distinctive feature of this service is that it enjoys a monopoly of coercion. That is the necessary condition for the conduct of the business; any division of authority would defeat the purpose for which Government is set up. Yet, the fact remains that Government is a human organization, consisting of men who are exactly like the men they serve. That is, they too seek to satisfy their desires with the minimum of exertion, and they too are insatiable in their appetites. In addition to the run-of-the-mill desires which possess all men, Government personnel acquire one peculiar to their occupation: the adulation showered on them because they alone exercise coercion. They are people apart.

The honorifics that stem from the exercise of power arouse a passion for power, particularly with men whose capacities would go quite unnoticed in the market place, and the temptation is strong to expand the area of power; the negative function of protection is too confining for men of ambition. The tendency then in the world of officialdom is to assume a capacity for positive functions, to invade the market place, to undertake to regulate, control, manage, and manipulate its techniques. In point of fact, it does nothing of the kind, since the techniques are self-operating, and all that political power can accomplish by its interventions is to control human behavior; it effects compliance by the threat of physical punishment. That, indeed, is the be-all and end-all of political power. Yet, such is the makeup of the human that he looks up to, and sometimes worships, the fellow human who dominates his will, and it is this acquired sense of superiority that is the principal profit of officialdom.

The transition from negative Government to positive State is marked by the use of political power for predatory purposes. In its pursuit of power, officialdom takes into consideration the ineluctable something-for-nothing passion, and proceeds to win the support of segments of Society bent on feathering their nests without picking feathers. It is a *quid pro quo* arrangement, by which the power of compulsion is sublet to favored individuals or groups in return for their acquiescence to the acquisition of power. The State sells privilege, which is nothing but an economic advantage gained by some at the expense of others. In olden times, the privileged group were a land-owning class, who furnished military support for political power, or a mercantilist group, who contributed to the imperial coffers out of their politically generated monopoly profits; with the advent of popular suffrage, making political preferment dependent on wider favor, the business of bribery had to be extended, and so came the subsidization of farmers, tenants, the aged, users of electric power, and so on. Their vested interest in the State makes them amenable to its purposes.

It is this partnership in predation that characterizes the State. Without the support of privileged groups the State would collapse. Without the State the privileged groups would disappear. The contract is rooted in the law of parsimony.

The instrument that puts the State into a bargaining position with its favorites is taxation. In the beginning, when the simple community sets up Government, it is admitted that its operatives cannot be productive and therefore have to be supported by the maket place. Services must be paid for. But the manner of paying for Government service poses a problem: taxes are compulsory charges, not voluntary payments, and their collection has to be entrusted to the very people who live by them; the compulsory power entrusted to them is used in the collection of their own wages. That this function should be pursued with vigor is understandable. Yet, where political power is under the constant surveillance of Society, the urgency to increase taxes for the purpose of enlarging political power can be held in leash. But this restraint loses potency as Society grows in size and in complexity of interests; the preoccupation of its members with productive enterprise dims their interest in public affairs, which tend to become the private concern of officials. Centralization of political power, which is merely its release from the restraint of social sanctions, ensues, and tax levies grow apace. The political establishment—the court of Louis XIV or the equally nonproductive bureaucracy of the modern "welfare" State—thus acquires self-sufficiency; it has the wherewithal to meet its enforcement payroll and to invest in power-accumulating enterprises.

There is always good and sufficient reason for more and more taxes. Solomon's temple, the roads of Rome, the rearing of "infant industries," military preparedness, the regulation of morals, the improvement of the "general welfare"—all call for drafts on the market place, and the end-product of each draft is an increase in the power of the

State. Some of the appropriations seep through to some members of Society, thus satisfying the something-for-nothing urge, at least temporarily, and so stimulate a disposition to tolerate the institution and to obliterate understanding of its predatory character. Until the State reaches its ultimate objective, absolutism, its answer to tax-grumbling is that the "other fellow" pays all the levies and that seems to satisfy.

Pushing on fast through the biography of political institutions, the practice of buying the support of privileged and subsidized groups sloughs off when the State becomes self-sufficient; that is, when the market place is completely under its domination. The State then becomes the only privileged class. Custom and necessity reduce Society to a condition of subservience to the bureaucracy and the police, the components of the State. This condition is currently known as totalitarianism, but it is in fact nothing but conquest, the conquest of Society by the State. So that, whether or not the State originated in conquest, as some historians hold, the end result of unchecked political institutions is the same: Society is enslaved.

The end is not yet. The stature of the State grows by predation, the stature of Society shrinks in proportion. For an explanation for this antithesis we return to the composition of man. We find that he works only to satisfy his desires, of which he has a plenitude, that his output of effort is in proportion to his intake of satisfactions. If his investment of labor yields no profit, or if experience tells him none can be expected, his interest in laboring flags. That is, production declines by the amount of expropriation he must endure; if expropriation is severe enough and evasion becomes impossible, so that he learns to accept it as a way of life and forgets what it actually is, his output tends to the minimum of mere existence. But, since the State thrives on what it expropriates, the general decline in production which it induces by its avarice foretells its own doom. Its source of income dries up. Thus, in pulling Society down it pulls itself down. Its ultimate collapse is usually occasioned by a disastrous war, but preceding that event is a history of increasing and discouraging levies on the market place, causing a decline in the aspirations, hopes and self-esteem of its victims.

When we speak of the disappearance of a civilization we do not mean that a people has been extinguished. Every holocaust leaves survivors. What is implied by the fall of a civilization is the disappearance from memory of an accumulation of knowledge and of values that once obtained among a people. The prevailing arts and sciences, the religion and manners, the ways of living and of making a living have been forgotten. They have been obliterated not by a pile of dust but by a general lack of interest in marginal satisfactions, in the things men strive to achieve when the struggle for existence is won. One can manage to get along without knives and forks when the getting of food is trouble enough, and the first business of raiment is to provide warmth, not adornment. Contrariwise, as the primary necessaries accumulate, the human begins to dream of new worlds to conquer, including the world of the mind—culture, ideas, values. The accumulating conquests become the indicia of a civilization. The loss of a civilization is the reverse of that process of cultural accumulation. It is the giving up, as a matter of necessity, of those satisfactions that are not essential to existence. It is a process of forgetting through force of circumstance; it is abstinence imposed by environment. Sometimes nature will for a while impose abstinence, but the record shows that man is quite capable of overcoming such obstacles to his ambitions. The obstacle he does not seem able to overcome is his inclination to predation, which gives rise to the institution of the State; it is this institution that ultimately induces a climate of uselessness, of lack of interest in striving, and thus destroys the civilization it feeds upon. Or so the record shows : every civilization that declined or was lost carried an all-powerful State on its back.

    Collapse of a State means a weakening of the instruments of coercion by means of which property in the fruits of one's labors was transferred to nonproducing rulership or its supporting accomplices. Thereafter, maybe for centuries, freedom prevails, men learn to dream and hope again, and the realization of each dream through effort encourages further fantasy and generates more effort; thus wealth multiplies, knowledge accumulates, manners take shape, and the non-material values attain importance in man's hierarchy. A new civilization is born. Although something of the lost civilization is recaptured by accident, what is dug up has to be relearned; the new civilization does not grow out of its predecessor, but emerges from the efforts of the living. At any rate, history tells us, a civilization no more than gets started when a political institution attaches itself to it, feeds on it, and in the end devours it. And the roundelay starts all over again.

    Is there no escape from the cycle? None has as yet been discovered. Nevertheless, the search for a formula for the "good society" has never been abandoned, hope being what it is, and out of the laboratory of the human mind has come a congeries of utopias. The connotation of unreality that the word has acquired follows from the fact that every utopia ignores the central operating lever of man: he seeks to satisfy his desires with the least expenditure of effort. Every "good society" conjured up by philosophers and reformers presupposes an imaginary man managing his behavior by the dictates of pure reason and keeping in mind the long-range effects of his every act. Since there is no such man, or none we know of, every utopian scheme is indulgently put into the category of a fairy tale, interesting but unreal.

To be sure, man is a reasoning animal, and if he were to refer the matter to his reason he would conclude that some-thing-for-nothing is an impossibility; what one acquires "for free" must be provided by another. He would admit that a Society consisting entirely of consumers, say pirates, could not exist. He would concede without argument that production must precede consumption, that the purpose of production is consumption, that nothing would be produced if there were no prospect of enjoyment. He need not be an economist to arrive at such conclusions. All that, he would say, is common sense.

Yet, how easily does common sense take flight before the prospect of a gratuity or an unearned profit! Reason is not lacking in sufficient logic to circumvent reason when a handout is involved. The beneficiary finds nothing incongruous in a regimen of "bread and circuses"; here is visible evidence that something-for-nothing is not a mirage. Is it cold logic that generates an urgency for "protective" tariffs or a passion for getting more than one gives? When the State undertakes to provide "cheap" electricity for one section of the population at the expense of another, there are reasoners enough to support the arrangement. The libraries are full of tomes justifying subsidies of all sorts, and leveling—or the forcible taking from one to give to another—has long been the favorite preoccupation of professorial brains. Aristotle, the peer of logicians, found a syllogism to support the oldest form of exploitation known to man.

Yes, man is endowed with the gift of reason, but he is also possessed of appetites and an aversion to labor, and too often his reason bends to his other characteristics. The failure of utopians to accept this fact, or to accept man as he is, not as he ought to be, gives their schemes a dreamlike quality.

Generally speaking, utopianism falls into two main categories: the anarchistic and the communistic. The one posits as its primary premise the essential reasonableness and goodness of man, which are perverted by the introduction of force. It is the policeman, says the anarchist, who makes the criminal; remove the one and the other disappears. The communistic utopian, on the other hand, puts all the blame for social disorder on the institution of private property; abolish that institution (with or without force, according to the utopians conceit), and the "good society" will follow as a matter of course. (Incidentally, most anarchistic utopians would also abolish private property by the very force they decry; apparently, force is commendable when it is used by the right person for the right purpose.) The anarchistic premise, that the policeman came before and made the thief, is lacking in historical support; the sheriff came only because cattle rustling called for him. The communistic premise, that private property is the root of all social evil, assumes that man works for the sake of working, and without regard for the prospect of possession and enjoyment. Neither premise coincides with observable experience, and therefore the syllogisms built on each hangs in the mid-air of unreality.

Significantly, all utopian programs pay considerable attention to the political organization of man. The philosophic anarchist (relying on the perfectibility of man through education) is convinced that when the individual comes to his senses he will not need or tolerate the State. The communist believes that an all-powerful State is necessary not only for the wiping out of private property but also of the inclination of the individual to own, and expects that instrument to "wither away" when it has accomplished that purpose. Then there are the utopians who dwell somewhere between these schools; accepting the State as a desirable or unavoidable fact of life (or even enjoying divine sanction), they propose to rid it of its admitted imperfections by legalistic tinkering; *The Republic* of Plato is the best known of this type. All utopias are characterized by an avoidance of the fact that the State is made by man and in his own image, that if he were not constantly on the prowl for something-for-nothing he would never build such an institution.

Some indirect recognition of the fact that the State is the image of man, or vice versa, is found in those Utopias that lay claim to scientific exactitude. Beginning with a theory that is nothing but an unproven hypothesis, they do pretty well in endowing the State with a socially beneficial character. The theory holds that man is not a reasoning animal, or even a thinking one, and is certainly without fixed or immutable instincts; his behavior consists entirely of reflex actions induced by environmental conditioning. From this premise (which its proponents accept as axiomatic) it follows that man will be what his environmental influences compel him to be, and that the "perfect" man will emerge from the "perfect" environment. It is the mold that makes the man. If, therefore, we would improve the condition of man we must apply ourselves to the improvement of the mold into which this bit of protoplasm is to be poured.

But how and by whom is this mold to be built? It is admittedly a colossal job, which only the State with its monopoly of power is capable of performing. But the State itself is a human institution, and the question arises as to the capacity of the nonthinking human to put the State on the job of producing the "perfect" environment. The "scientists" get themselves out of this logical quandary by simply putting their basic theory aside for the moment and admitting, at least tacitly, that *some* people are in fact capable of thinking. For an as-yet-unexplained reason, these "scientists" have been able to free themselves from *their* environmental influences and are actually capable of cerebration; for that reason they have been chosen (by themselves, of course, since nobody else is capable of passing judgment on their capacities) to draw up the blueprint for the "perfect" environment which, by use of its force, the State can effectuate. Certainty of success will be assured by entrusting the power to the "scientists." And we who cannot think are for that very reason estopped from questioning either their logic or the soundness of their utopia.

Is utopia—the "good society"—an impossibility? One would be rash indeed to say so categorically. Yet, anyone who speculates on mans ability to put his social life in perfect order must take into account the biological fact of longevity. Man seeks to satisfy his desires while he lives, not when death has cut short his appetites, and actuarial figures tell him just about how long he may expect to live. His pattern of behavior is necessarily determined by his expectancy. Which is to say that in the nature of things his is a short-run view, although his perspective may be lengthened by a concern for the welfare of his immediate posterity, his children and grandchildren in being. Beyond that there is the "future of his country," a speculative interest that can have little bearing on his day-to-day chores.

The banker knows full well that the State's bonds in his vaults do not represent goods produced but are merely claims on production; the "interest" they yield is taxes, draughts on the market place, and he is in fact a tax collector once removed. Nor is he unaware of the inflationary character of these pieces of paper: that in the long run they depreciate the value of all his assets as well as those of his depositors, that the market place is indeed impoverished by his holdings. What's more, if he stops to think about it, he must know that the more of these bonds he holds the more he must support the fiscal activities of the State, for depreciation of the value of these bonds could put him out of business. Prudence compels him to disregard such considerations; he cooperates with the State's financing schemes, even if he suspects that in doing so he will gradually be downgraded to a secretarial position. In his need for showing a profit this year he puts aside whatever scruples he may have about buying the State's bonds. The future must take care of itself.

The corporation president has become accustomed to a standard of living calling for a certain income. He likes it and so does his wife. It is true that he has earned three times that amount and that the State has confiscated two thirds of his earnings. He resents the confiscation, wishes he could retain more and thus improve his standard, but finds it convenient to go along with the State for good reason. Perhaps his corporation is wholly or partly in the employ of the State; in that case, his income is actually derived from the taxes he is forced to pay. It is true that his employees in the aggregate pay more than he does and, though he has not figured it out, the probability is that he senses a profit in this allocation of taxes. Perhaps, if they were not taxed, his employees would buy the corporation's products as liberally as does the tax collector, but selling to a multitude of buyers would entail more sales and credit problems, and for the time being (which is all he is interested in) he finds it easier to do business with the One Big Buyer. He hires a lobbyist to do his selling.

Continuing with the corporation president, if the sales of his product drop to a point where his accustomed profits are threatened—say because taxes have deprived his prospective customers of purchasing power—he is inclined to look with favor on the State's inflationary activities. The distribution of more money, even though slightly counterfeit, will temporarily enrich the populace and enable them to make his sales chart good to look at. That the infusion of new money into the market place will have the effect of depreciating the value of his eroding plant, possibly to the extent of putting his business in an insolvent condition, no matter how much he may put aside for replacement, is a consideration, to be sure; but that is something for the next president and the stockholders of the future to worry about. This year he must pay dividends.*

It would be a stupid farmer indeed who did not realize that being paid for not producing is an anomaly; it would be an insensitive one who did not resent the regulations that accompany the largess. Yet the immediate need for a tractor or television set obliterates such considerations, including the probability that his son will never be an independent farmer. The subsidized renter may see some connection between his privilege and the deductions from his pay envelope; even so, it is nice to know that his quarters cost him less than does the comparable habitation of his nonsubsidized neighbor. The old lady living on "social security" remittances, the veteran whose doctor bill is taken care of by the State, and the malingerer receiving unemployment gratuities are not in the least concerned with the future. Even the philosopher who sees dire forebodings in the trend makes peace with it, if necessity demands, and in the comfort of an unearned grant finds solace for his misgivings. We are condemned to live in the present.

It is this biological necessity that robs the long-term point of view of reality and facilitates the operations of the State. The need of living now bends the will to live to the conditions under which living is possible; just as a man patterns his life in the wilderness to primitive conditions, so does he make adjustment to the rules, regulations, controls, confiscations, and interventions imposed on him by political power. If these restraints on his aspirations are regularized, so that his "way of life" achieves a semblance of stability, he soon loses consciousness of restraint; what he may have resented at the beginning is not only accepted but also defended. For such is the composition of man that his adjustment to environment is not confined to mere physical, insensate accommodation; it must include a conscious acceptance, a justification, a moral support. He cannot live comfortably without giving his blessing to the conditions under which he lives. His competence with words aids the process of accommodation; with words he develops an ideology that satisfies his mind as to the correctness and even righteousness of his "way of life." This is the secret ally of the State—the inclination of the human to adore the conditions which have been imposed on him and under which he has found a comfortable adjustment. Its propaganda machinery, by constant reiteration, turns the ideological phrases into a liturgy; its bureaucracy, which regularizes the cherished "way of life," acquires the glory of a priesthood; its buildings, even its prisons, are covered with a distinctive aura; its formalism becomes ritualistic, its utterances oracular. Only the theoretician, the economist and the historian, concerns himself with the long-term consequences of the State's interventions. In the meantime one must live, and in the meantime "long live the king."

In these circumstances, the long-termer, the prophet who harps on first principles and the ultimate consequences of violation, is a dealer in unreality and an unwanted disturber of the adjustment. His vagaries may be remembered and his prophecy recalled when at long last his forebodings have come to pass. That is, when the restraints multiply to the point where adjustment leaves little area for living, when a miserable existence is all that one can get out of one's efforts. It is then that the primordial instinct for freedom looms larger than the instinct for life itself and there is nothing left to do but to throw off the shackles of the State. But that, for the present, is in the unrealistic realm of the long-term.

The instinct for freedom, the yearning for self-expression without let or hindrance, is the stuff of which utopia is made. Were it not for that element in unscrutable man's makeup he would never be involved in political matters and his history would be like unto a history of the jungle. Man, the producer, must have freedom, while man, the predator, puts limitations on freedom, and this inner dichotomy is the plot of his life story. His search for the "good society" is his search for a denouement. Whether or not it is in the nature of things that the struggle should go on indefinitely, he cannot help trying his hand at fashioning a happy ending. And what follows herewith is simply another attempt at the same thing.

The principal ingredient in any formula for the "good society" must be a preventive. How can Society protect itself against the tendency of political power to encroach upon and liquidate social power? This has been the continuing problem of social integrations, and the only solution human ingenuity has hit upon is surveillance and supervision. Society must always keep its eyes on and, when need be, lay its hands on political power. In practice, surveillance and supervision take the form of constitutionalism, or written limitations on political power, with popular suffrage the enforcement agency. Experience shows, however, that constitutions and suffrage only delay, do not prevent, the fermentation of political power; men can and do vote themselves into its clutches under the promise of an unearned advantage, and constitutions are not written in the indelible ink of natural law. The fallibility of constitutionalism lies in the fact that as political power extends its area of operations it is able to play one group against another, catering to their diverse cupidities, and under cover of such intrasocial conflicts (class struggles) its inherent proclivity for expansion breaks through the constitutional bounds. There is the further fact that production, not surveillance and supervision of political power, is the first business of Society, and that this ancillary occupation is likely to be overlooked; particularly so when those who exercise power are beyond the personal purview of those upon whom it is exercised. As a practical matter, therefore, surveillance and supervision are an effective restraint only when the political unit is small, so small that the political personnel cannot escape social pressures. That is, the town-hall type of Government.

We are speaking of the political, not the economic, unit. The size of the economic unit is always determined by the radius of exchanges, and is always regulated by the human sense of value. Buyer and seller, regardless of the distance between them, either in space or culture, become members of the market place by the act of exchange. The market place is self-regulatory, operating under laws which are self-enforcing and carry their own sanctions; it is a mechanism which functions without the use of political power and whose efficiency can only be lowered by the injection of that power. It will be as large as customers and sellers want it to be. Without political interference it can be world-wide.

The best that political power can do in the premises is to prevent theft (including the violation of contract), and this it can do only by punishing the thief after the act has been committed, with the hope that such punishment will discourage repetition or emulation. Even in this function it is less effective than social sanctions; exile from the market place of a community unable or unwilling to keep its house in order, or of an individual who establishes a reputation for dishonesty, is retribution enough. If it is in the economic interest of any political unit to maintain police relations with other communities, liaison through representatives can be established, but the powers and functions of these representatives must be held within the purview of their employers, the local town-hall meeting. Political power can and will be put to antisocial practices only when those to whom it is entrusted act as principals, not as agents.

The means by which the political person—"divine right" king or elected official—achieves independent stature is the power to appropriate property. Without appropriation there cannot be a State, and the power of the State is in direct proportion to the amount of property it appropriates. Contrariwise, social power is measurable by the amount of property the individual producer is able to retain and dispose of as he sees fit. The State thrives on taxation, Society suffers from it. The difference between a free Society and a dominated one is in the percentage of property the State lays its hands on.

All taxes are compulsory exactions—"voluntary taxation" is a contradiction in terms—and the problem that Society must face, if it would retain its freedom, is whether it will keep the compulsory power in its own hands, under strict surveillance, or transfer it to its political agents. Transference carries with it the relinquishment of social power and the enlargement of political power, or the deterioration of the negative Government into the positive State. Hence, the safeguard of the "good society," or the means by which it can be achieved, is the constant, rigorous, and jealous examination of every tax request, and the careful supervision of the disbursement of the levies. Above all, the politician must never be given blanket authority to impose taxes; each tax proposal must be considered on its own merits, as a temporary levy intended for a specific purpose, even as the individual manages his own economy. Thus, if a road is to be built, the cost should be provided for by a tax that terminates when the road is completed; if war is forced on a people, the taxing power should be granted for the duration only. The ideal of the "good society" is the abolition of all taxes, but that presupposes the existence of the "perfect" man and a general understanding of how public expense can be met without levying on production; until that time comes, if ever, the best that Society can do to protect itself is to keep a suspicious eye on all taxation.

The proposal to keep political power so decentralized that it cannot escape the vigilance of social power rests its case on the assumption that the highest value in mans hierarchy is freedom. Does he put it above all other desires? Even material satisfactions? If so, what does he mean by freedom? The definition that quickly suggests itself is "absence of restraint." The lone frontiersman had plenty of that kind of freedom and found it wanting; he was quite willing to part with some of it in exchange for the higher wages that came from cooperation with others. But cooperation entails an obligation, that of shaping one's behavior to the wishes of others, of considering public opinion both in one's occupation and in one's deportment. So then, freedom in Society is not the absence of restraints, but the management of one's affairs by a code of self-governance. The price of the benefits of cooperation is self-restraint.

In particular, the obligation imposed by freedom in Society is respect for the privacy of property. When the frontiersman worked for himself, directly, he concerned himself with property only when a marauding animal or stray human threatened his ownership. He had a keen interest in holding on to the things he produced—because of his labor investment—and kept his firearm ready to assure him of possession. But the concept of property rights assumed significant meaning when through the mechanism of the market place abundances and accumulations made their appearance. It is at this point that self-governance is put to the test. Why? Because man seeks to satisfy his desires with the minimum of exertion. The same urgency was upon him when he worked alone, but the best he could do about it was to devise some rudimentary short cuts or labor-saving instruments. When the cooperative social organism grows up around him and abundances appear, the thought occurs to him that perhaps the satisfaction of desires at no expenditure of labor is an attainable goal. The something-for-nothing impulse that is imbedded in his makeup sometimes gets beyond the bounds of self-restraint. At this point, or in expectation of its coming, the common concern for property gives rise to a compact among the members of Society; external restraints on the inner urge are set up. Government is an admission that the "absence of restraint" is inconsistent with freedom.

It might be argued that reason should tell the individual there is no such thing as something-for-nothing, that somebody has to labor to provide satisfactions, that the condition necessary for general abundance is security of possession. In fact, reason might put him in the way of a principle: that production alone can raise the level of wages, that expropriation tends to lower it. But, taking him by and large, man does not always act on principle; more often, he acts on considerations of immediate profit and convenience. Reason seems to be less of a guide for human behavior than appetite. His history supplies plenty of support for this opinion. Even in the smallest and most intimate social unit, the family, the predatory impulse finds expression in the Jacob-Esau inheritance swindle, and the use of fraud or force to acquire property without laboring for it is the leitmotiv of the social saga. Were it not for this dominant element in man's makeup, conquest would never have been practiced, slavery would never have been known, privileged classes would never have made an appearance, monopolies never instituted and the "welfare state" never thought of. Indeed, there never would have been a State, which is merely the organization of force for the transference of property from "one set of pockets to another."

Freedom is not the highest in man's hierarchy of values. He may talk of it in the most laudatory terms, but his behavior belies his protestations. Although at times, when the multiplication of external restraints makes existence unbearable, he does put forth effort to shake off some of the shackles, his over-all biography indicates an overpowering passion for something-for-nothing, an inability or unwillingness to hold it in leash, and a readiness to submit to restraints under the promise of loot. The modern "welfare state" is most illustrative; it is admittedly and boastfully the organization of force for the confiscation and distribution of property. It is the complete antithesis of that "absence of restraint" which is the substance of freedom. Despite this bald fact, it acquires a reputation for humanitarianism and receives the blessing of all who batten on the production of others as well as of those who hope to: the banker and the industrialist who thrive on the taxes it collects, the farmer who is paid for not farming, the "free lunch" mother, the host of pleaders for special privilege. Is it freedom they want? Hardly. The responsibilities of freedom are in conflict with the law of parsimony.

One last word, for Americans who have a penchant for the long run and hope "to do something about it." Supporting that hope is the still-green memory of a Society that managed its affairs with a minimum of external restraint. Even though the American State has gone a long way toward establishing its dominance over American Society, it is still in contention with the folklore of freedom, and it may be possible to impede the progress of the State by invoking this tradition. After all, this is a young country; the record of its beginnings is still alive, while living men can recall the struggles of the State to attain its present position. If the original enthusiasm for freedom can be revived, it, may be possible to restrain political power before it completely engulfs social power. It is worth a try.

In the tradition, to begin with, there is the doctrine of states' rights. It is a decentralizing doctrine, intended to keep political power contained and off balance. Though it has been only rarely invoked since the formation of the Union, and then only for some specious and temporary purpose, its original idea of keeping political power under close surveillance and supervision has potency. It is in the interests of the political establishments of the separate states to prevent their engulfment by the central authority, even as in olden times the local chieftains kept a jealous eye on the growing power of the king. If this concern for local autonomy can be revived, the case for freedom will not be completely lost.

The drive toward centralization began long before the American State acquired the power to tax incomes, but this instrument provided the means for reducing the states to mere administrative subdivisions; for it gave the central authority the wherewithal to buy the subservience of local authorities. Hence, nothing can be done about restoring the balance between the two unless the Sixteenth Amendment to the Constitution is repealed.

But, while this political purpose demands repeal of the amendment, a far more fundamental reason calls for it. It is that the power to tax incomes violates the right of property, which underlies the sacred rights of "life, liberty and the pursuit of happiness." It is silly to talk of freedom as long as the State can and does lay its hands on the earnings of the producer; unless the individual has the prerogative of possession, enjoyment, and disposition of all his produce, without let or hindrance, his status is less than that of a freeman; the more of it that is taken from him the nearer he approaches the status of a slave. It is interesting to note that the amendment puts no limit on the amount the State may confiscate.

Therefore, if the progress of the American State toward the subjugation of American Society is to be stopped, its power to levy on incomes must be abolished. But that can be done only if absence-of-restraint takes precedence over something-for-nothing in the scale of human values. The will for freedom comes before freedom.

* In the classical economic tradition it was always the debtor class who asked for "cheap" money. We now find the industrialist and, at times, the financial crowd who look favorably on "controlled" inflation. This phenomenon is worth exploring.